The Young Velázquez

The Young Velázquez

The Education of the Virgin Restored

Essays by John Marciari,
Carmen Albendea, Ian McClure, Anikó Bezur, and Jens Stenger,
and Benito Navarrete Prieto

YALE UNIVERSITY ART GALLERY
NEW HAVEN

DISTRIBUTED BY YALE UNIVERSITY PRESS
NEW HAVEN AND LONDON

Publication made possible by a
generous grant from Banco Santander.

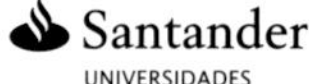 Santander
UNIVERSIDADES

First published in 2014 by the
Yale University Art Gallery
P.O. Box 208271
New Haven, CT 06520-8271
artgallery.yale.edu/publications

Distributed by
Yale University Press
302 Temple Street
P.O. Box 209040
New Haven, CT 06520-9040
yalebooks.com/art

Published in conjunction with the exhibition
*El joven Velázquez: "La educación de la Virgen"
de Yale restaurada*, organized by the Instituto de la
Cultura y las Artes de Sevilla (ICAS) and the Yale
University Art Gallery.

NO8DO
AYUNTAMIENTO DE SEVILLA

Espacio Santa Clara, Instituto de la Cultura y
las Artes de Sevilla (ICAS)
October 15, 2014–January 15, 2015

Tiffany Sprague, Director of Publications
and Editorial Services

Christopher Sleboda, Director of Graphic Design

Translators: Vajra Kilgour, Jacqueline Tornell,
and Rosario Albendea

Set in Monotype Garamond type
Printed at GHP, West Haven, Conn.

Jacket illustration: Diego Velázquez, detail of the
Education of the Virgin (pl. 1)

Library of Congress Cataloging-in-Publication Data
The young Velázquez : "The education of
the Virgin" restored / John Marciari, Carmen
Albendea, Ian McClure, Anikó Bezur, Jens Stenger,
and Benito Navarrete Prieto.
     pages cm
   Includes bibliographical references.
   ISBN 978-0-300-20786-6 (paperback)
   1. Velázquez, Diego, 1599–1660. *Education of the
Virgin*—Exhibitions. 2. Mary, Blessed Virgin,
Saint—Art—Exhibitions. 3. Anne (Mother
of the Virgin Mary), Saint—Art—Exhibitions.
4. Painting, Spanish—Conservation and
restoration—Connecticut—New Haven—
Exhibitions. I. Marciari, John. Young Velázquez.
II. Navarrete Prieto, Benito. *Education of the Virgin*
and the shaping of early naturalism. III. Title:
Education of the Virgin.
   ND813.V4A675 2014
   759.6—dc23
                                    2014019297

10 9 8 7 6 5 4 3 2 1

Contents

Director's Foreword

The opportunity to redesign, renovate, and reinstall the three-building complex that is now the Yale University Art Gallery brought with it, a little over ten years ago, an equally important opportunity to review and reconsider nearly the entirety of our historic collections, now numbering in excess of 200,000 works of art. Fresh pairs of curatorial eyes examined paintings, sculptures, and decorative objects, many of which had not been considered with adequate attention to their qualities or blemishes in generations, in some cases not for a century or more. Many wonderful discoveries emerged from this process. Paintings by Fra Angelico, Paolo Uccello, Titian, and van Dyck that we knew we owned but had not realized were by these stellar masters, and others by Bellotto, Stubbs, Linnel, or Cabanel that had always been fully recognized but never much appreciated, now have pride of place on the walls in our permanent-collection galleries. But none of these pleasant surprises can compare to the amazement we all felt when it was proposed to us that the beautiful but damaged *Education of the Virgin* that had long been inventoried in our storerooms as "anonymous Spanish, seventeenth century," might actually be the earliest-known major altarpiece by Diego Velázquez, a discovery that caused a flurry of excitement and debate when it was announced publicly in the summer of 2010.

The *Education of the Virgin* emerged slowly out of obscurity. Photographic records document its installation in the Yale School of the Fine Arts in the nineteenth century, hanging high on a wall amid an assortment of plaster casts as models for students to copy. More than one attempt to clean it was begun and abandoned over the first half of the twentieth century, but no serious attention was devoted to it until the winter of 2002–3, when Laurence Kanter, our newly appointed Lionel Goldfrank III Curator of European Art, placed it on a list of works of sufficiently high quality and interest to justify further study, cleaning, and restoration, and possible installation in the new galleries then being planned. Shortly afterward, John Marciari joined the Department of Early European Art as the Nina and Lee Griggs Associate Curator of European Art, and he quickly selected the *Education of the Virgin* from this "to-be-conserved" list as deserving of special attention. The rest of the story, as they say, is now history. There followed six years of research and preliminary conservation work, leading to John's publication of the painting four years ago, in 2010. The appearance of his article—after which we displayed the painting partially cleaned in our galleries—sparked a lively public debate that brought the painting to the attention of specialists and amateurs worldwide.

It was at this point that Banco Santander approached us with the exceedingly generous offer of sponsoring the complete conservation of the *Education of the Virgin*, fully aware of how complicated and involved a project this would be. It was their unflinching support that enabled our Susan Morse Hilles Chief Conservator, Ian McClure, to engage the services of Carmen Albendea to collaborate with him in bringing this ambitious project to a positive and timely conclusion, transforming an imposing but scarred and difficult-to-read canvas into that which we now believe it to be: a monument of the emerging genius of the greatest painter of Spain's Golden Age, Diego Velázquez. Their work, not only in recovering the hidden beauties of this captivating painting but also in drawing on and adding to the wealth of physical information available about Velázquez's technique in his early Sevillian period, is carefully detailed in their essay in this catalogue and will surely remain a fundamental contribution to Velázquez studies for a long time to come.

Finally, it is crucial to acknowledge the erudition and the infectious enthusiasm of our colleague in Seville, Benito Navarrete Prieto, whose tenacious determination to restore the *Education of the Virgin* to its rightful place in the canon of classical Spanish art as well as in the cultural legacy of his adoptive home is truly the genesis of this unique exhibition and catalogue. His hospitality, eloquence, and passionate commitment, all supported without wavering by the mayor of Seville and his entire cultural staff, made the hypothetical possibility of our collaboration a reality. I am sure I speak for the entire staff of the Yale University Art Gallery, for our Governing Board, and for the President and Officers of the University when I say that this is a collaboration of which we are, and will long be, most proud.

Jock Reynolds
The Henry J. Heinz II Director
Yale University Art Gallery

Mayor's Foreword

Between June 1 and June 20, 1620, Mother Jerónima de la Fuente was staying in the Sevillian convent of Santa Clara while waiting to set sail for Manila, where she was to found a new convent of Santa Clara. During this time, our most brilliant and world-famous artist, Diego Velázquez, visited the Sevillian convent and made a portrait of her, precisely in the space where we are now hosting this exhibition.

My words here today, besides expressing my elation, express gratitude. First, for having been able to bring the *Education of the Virgin* to Seville, from the prestigious institution Yale University; undoubtedly, for scholars of Velázquez this has been one of the most gratifying surprises and discoveries in recent years. Second, because one of the first paintings to emerge from Velázquez's brush is returning, even if only for a few months, to the city where he was born and trained, and where he left the first marks of his genius and mastery—which, in works like this, are expressed in the intimacy that results from the naturalistic details and from his training with Francisco Pacheco and others. There is also another significant circumstance: the scant distance between the convent of Santa Clara and the convent of Santa Ana, of the Shod Carmelites, for which this canvas was probably painted, precisely in the years when Velázquez was embarking upon his first works as a young artist, which testify to

early naturalism and are of the same stature as works that were being produced around the period between 1617 and 1620 in European capitals such as Rome and Antwerp.

I would also like to express my gratitude for the decisive collaboration of Banco Santander, and especially the perseverance of Paloma Botín and Salvador Medina; keenly aware of the significance and novelty of this new work in Velázquez's brilliant oeuvre, they took a gamble on collaborating with Yale on the restoration, study, and publication of the scientific results arising from the subsequent research. This work has taken over two years and is being presented in Seville as something truly exceptional, as much for researchers as for the general public, disseminating the results of the scientific work, which is pivotal for all of society, and making it a part of the advancement of knowledge. Because of this, the people of Seville will be able to enjoy an emblematic work that was painted in our city, and scholars who specialize in Velázquez's paintings have another incentive to dig deeper into his early work, especially with regard to his technique: One of the objectives of the exhibition is to present the canvas precisely in the context in which it was painted, together with all of the technical findings gleaned during the process of restoration and that demonstrate its authorship and intrinsic quality. To this end, the exhibition shows what Velázquez saw and learned from his model, the *Education of the*

Virgin by Juan de Roelas, generously lent by the Museo de Bellas Artes de Sevilla, as well as what he was also assimilating from all of the innovations contained in the *Holy Family* by Luis Tristán, on loan from the Minneapolis Institute of Arts—an essential touchstone for studies of both early naturalism and Velázquez's artworks. Along with these works we are also exhibiting Velázquez's *Saint Ildefonso Receiving the Chasuble from the Virgin*, owned by the City Council of Seville, in an exciting meeting of two masterpieces by the Sevillian painter.

But none of this would have been possible without the active participation of Jock Reynolds, the Henry J. Heinz II Director of the Yale University Art Gallery, and Laurence Kanter, Chief Curator and the Lionel Goldfrank III Curator of European Art, who understood the importance of publicly exhibiting and recognizing the results in our city for both Velázquez and Seville. Their visit to our city hall and their enthusiasm for the project from the beginning, back in August 2011, have been among the main factors guaranteeing that the dream would become a reality with the findings we are now presenting, which highlight the restoration work carried out by Carmen Albendea and Ian McClure. Thanks to all of them for sharing their expertise with all of us, and for collaborating on this exciting project, which has made it possible for the *Education of the Virgin* to shine with its own light, for the study and delight of all lovers of art and culture, in the city where it was conceived, designed, and painted. I should extend my appreciation to the City Council Cultural Representative María del Mar Sánchez Estrella and the team at the Instituto de la Cultura y las Artes de Sevilla (ICAS) for their efforts and dedication to this project, which will allow the city to become, once again, a prominent bastion of cultural initiatives of international significance.

Juan Ignacio Zoido Álvarez
Mayor of Seville

Acknowledgments

Several individuals have contributed to the realization of this exhibition and its accompanying catalogue. Foremost are those who have steadily supported the project from its inception: Jock Reynolds, the Henry J. Heinz II Director, and Laurence Kanter, Chief Curator and the Lionel Goldfrank III Curator of European Art, both of the Yale University Art Gallery; Juan Ignacio Zoido Álvarez, mayor of Seville and President of the Instituto de la Cultura y las Artes de Sevilla (ICAS); and Emilio Botín, Executive Chairman, Salvador Medina, Global Director of Santander Universities, Global Division, Eduardo Garrido, Director of Santander Universities, and Francisco de Borja Baselga Canthal, Director General of the Foundation Banco Santander, all of Banco Santander.

The organizers of the exhibition and authors of the catalogue wish to express their gratitude to the Museo de Bellas Artes de Sevilla and the Minneapolis Institute of Arts for their generous loans.

For the past two years, the authors of the catalogue have worked seamlessly to present a cogent and comprehensive examination of Yale's *Education of the Virgin*. They owe their gratitude to colleagues and scholars who contributed their expertise.

John Marciari extends a special thanks to Virginia Brilliant, John and Mable Ringling Museum of Art; Timothy Clifford, National Galleries of Scotland; Sol García, *Ars Magazine*; Patricia Sherwin Garland, former Senior Paintings Conservator, Yale University Art Gallery; Laurence Kanter; Elise K. Kenney, Archivist, Yale University Art Gallery; Julia Marciari-Alexander, Walters Art Museum; Lorenzo Pericolo, University of Warwick; Fernando Rayón, *Ars Magazine*; Matthew Rutenberg; and Salvador Salort-Pons, Detroit Institute of Arts.

Carmen Albendea, Ian McClure, Anikó Bezur, and Jens Stenger extend a special thanks to the following colleagues who generously shared advice, data, and information: Frank Zuccari, Art Institute of Chicago; Wendy Crawford and Serena Urry, Cincinnati Art Museum; Anabel Morillo, Fundación Focus-Abengoa; Damon Conover, George Washington University and the National Gallery of Art, Washington, D.C.; Rocío Bruquetas Galán, Instituto del Patrimonio Cultural de España; Charlotte Hale and Evan Read, Metropolitan Museum of Art, New York; Bénédicte de Donker, Musée des Beaux-Arts d'Orléans; Laura Alba, Rocío y María Teresa Dávila, Inmaculada Echevarría, Gabriele Finaldi, Jaime García-Máiquez, Carmen Garrido, María Dolores Gayo, and Javier Portús Pérez, all at the Museo Nacional del Prado; Mireia Mestre Campà and Mireia Campuzano i Lerín, both at the Museu Nacional d'Art de Catalunya; Zahira Véliz Bomford, Museum of Fine Arts, Houston; Lorraine Maule, National

Galleries of Scotland; Ashok Roy and Larry Keith, both at the National Gallery, London; Muirne Lydon, National Gallery of Ireland; and Hilary Macartney, History of Art Department, University of Glasgow. At the Yale University Art Gallery, they thank the staff of the Conservation Department; Christopher Mir, Museum Technician, Visual Resources Department; and Elise K. Kenney, Archivist.

Benito Navarrete Prieto extends a special thanks to Teresa Laguna and Margarita López, Catedral de Sevilla; José Morón Borrego, Fotógrafo; Rocío García Carranza, Roberto Alonso Moral, and Anabel Morillo, Fundación Focus-Abengoa; Valme Muñoz, Rocío Izquierdo, and Ignacio Hermoso, Museo de Bellas Artes de Sevilla; José Roda Peña, Universidad de Sevilla; Basilio Rodríguez García, Olivares; and Jesús Urrea, Universidad de Valladolid.

At the Yale University Art Gallery, many staff members worked on the different aspects and logistics of this project: L. Lynne Addison, Registrar; Paola D'Agostino, the Nina and Lee Griggs Assistant Curator of European Art; Amy Dowe, Senior Associate Registrar; John ffrench, Director of Visual Resources; Pamela Franks, Deputy Director for Exhibitions, Programming, and Education and the Seymour H. Knox, Jr., Curator of Modern and Contemporary Art; Jessica Labbé, Deputy Director for Finance and Administration; Meghan Lynch, Museum Assistant, Department of European Art; Brian P. McGovern, Assistant Director of Advancement; Charlene Senical, Assistant Business Manager; and Jill Westgard, Deputy Director for Advancement.

The production of the catalogue benefitted from the expertise of Christopher Sleboda, Director of Graphic Design; Tiffany Sprague, Director of Publications and Editorial Services; and Stacey Wujcik, Assistant Editor.

The organization and the presentation of the exhibition at the Convento de Santa Clara in Seville would not have been possible without the following: María del Mar Sánchez Estrella, Deputy Mayor for Culture, Education, Sports, and Youth and Vice President of ICAS; María Eugenia Candil Cano, General Manager of the Department of Culture; Rosario Pérez Pérez, Manager; Rocío Guerra Macho, Head of the Administrative and Economic Department of ICAS; Marcos Fernández, Head of the Publishing Department of ICAS; and José Lucas Chaves Maza, Cultural Projects and Activities Manager. Special thanks go to Santiago Martínez-Vares Gigliotti, Communications Manager at the City of Seville Council; and Alberto Díaz, Chief of Staff, and Alegría Cardesa, Deputy Chief of Staff, both at the Mayor's Office of Seville.

At Banco Santander, Paloma Botín, Emanuela Magadlena Gidea, and Charo López are also gratefully acknowledged.

Plates

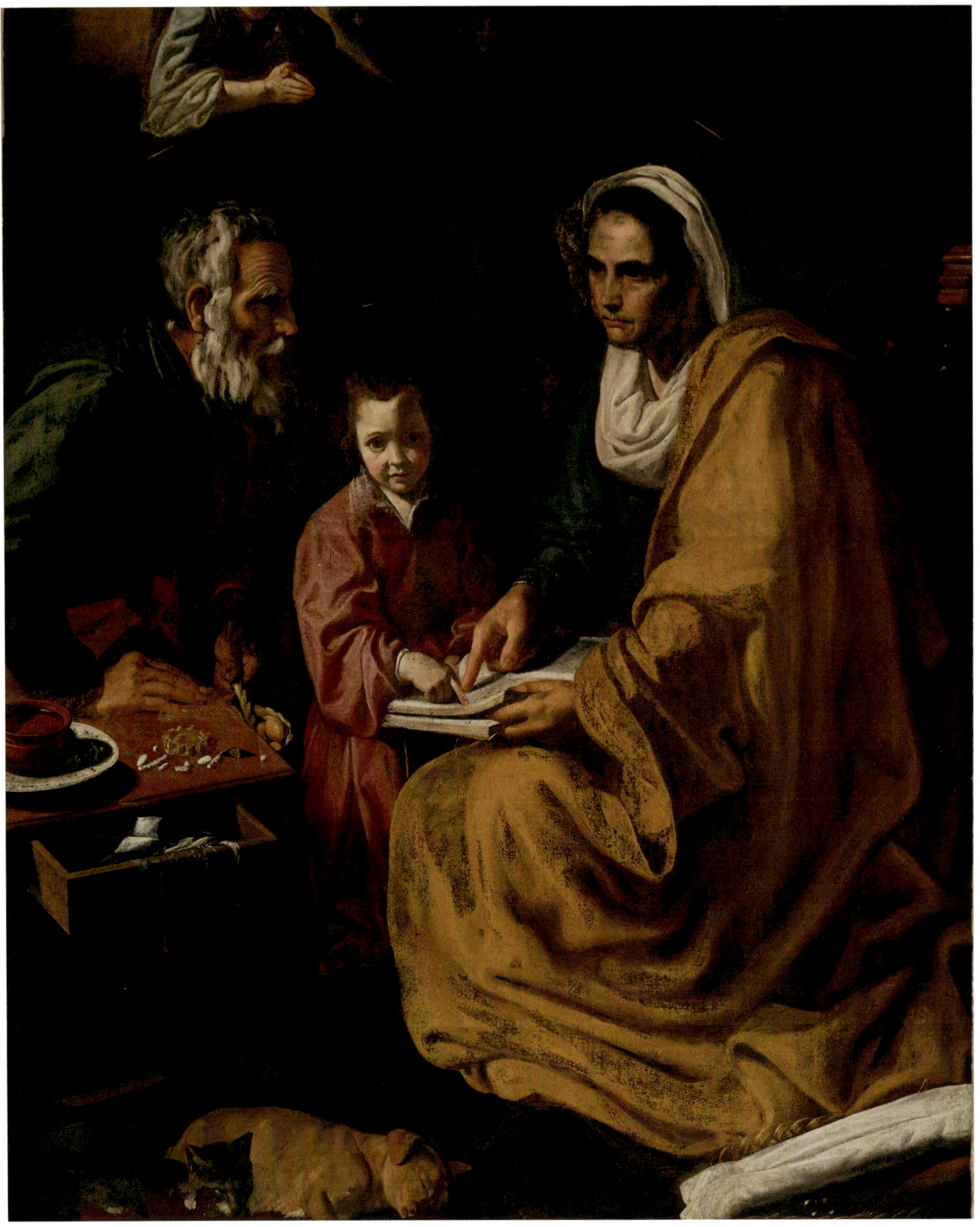

Pl. 1. Diego Velázquez, *The Education of the Virgin*, ca. 1617. Oil on canvas, 168 × 137 cm (66⅛ × 53¹⁵⁄₁₆ in.). Yale University Art Gallery, New Haven, Conn., Gift of Henry H. Townshend, B.A. 1897, LL.B. 1901, and Dr. Raynham Townshend, B.S. 1900S, inv. no. 1900.43

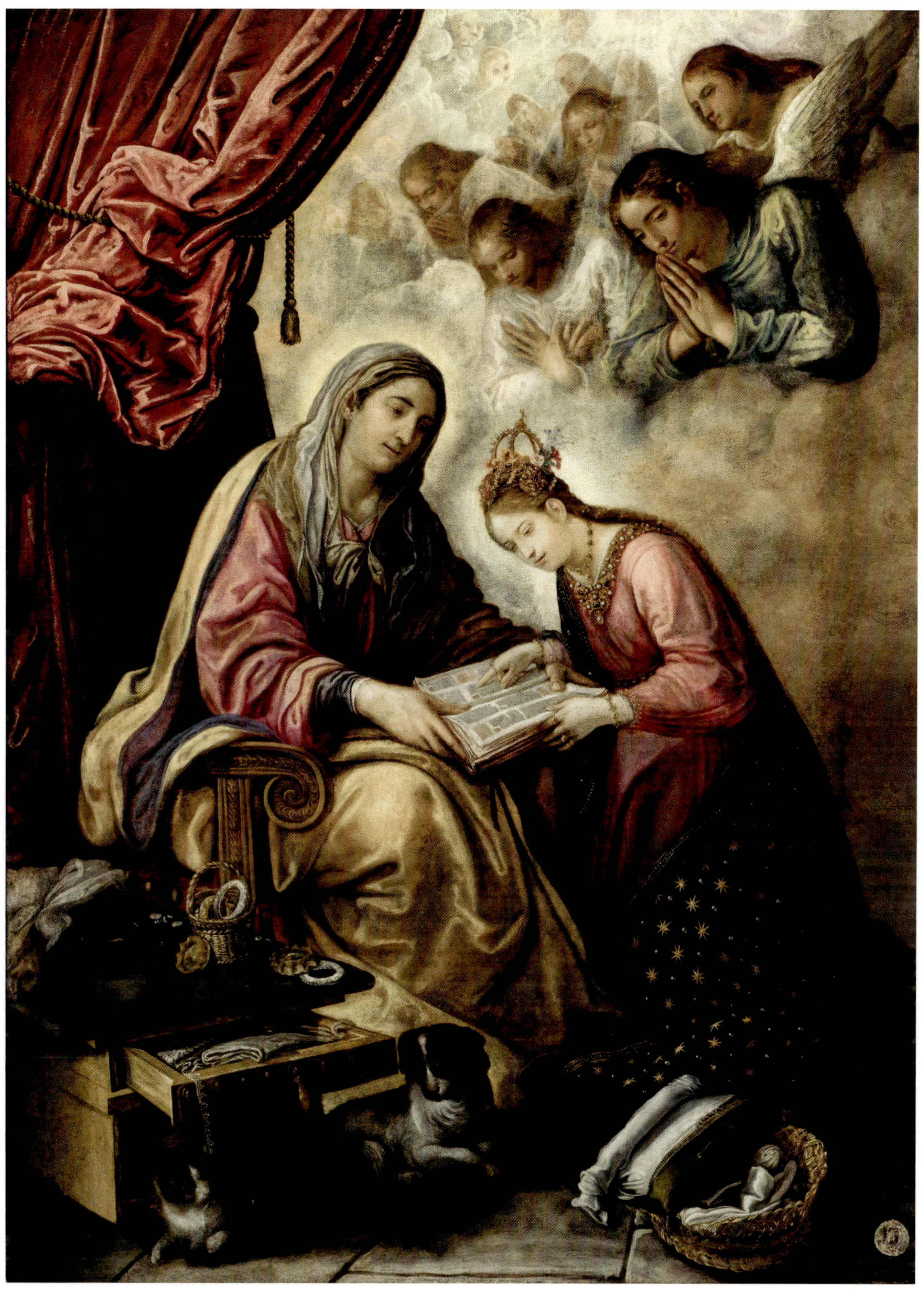

Pl. 2. Juan de Roelas, *The Education of the Virgin*, ca. 1612. Oil on canvas, 230 × 170 cm (7 ft. 6½ in. × 66¹⁵⁄₁₆ in.). Museo de Bellas Artes de Sevilla, inv. no. CE0134P

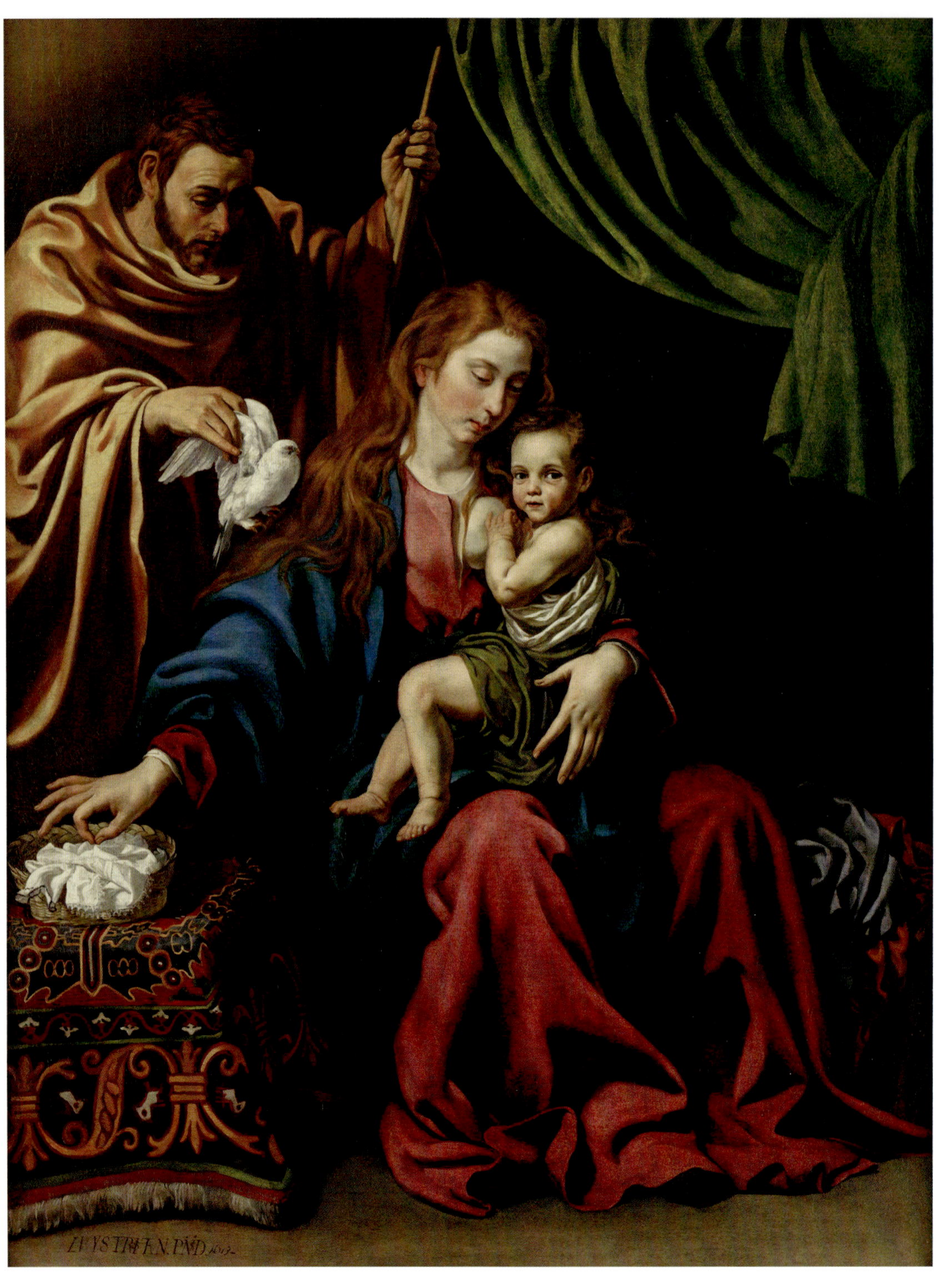

Pl. 3. Luis Tristán, *The Holy Family*, 1613. Oil on canvas, 142 × 109 cm (55¹⁵⁄₁₆ × 42¹⁵⁄₁₆ in.). Minneapolis Institute of Arts, The William Hood Dunwoody Fund, inv. no. 74.2

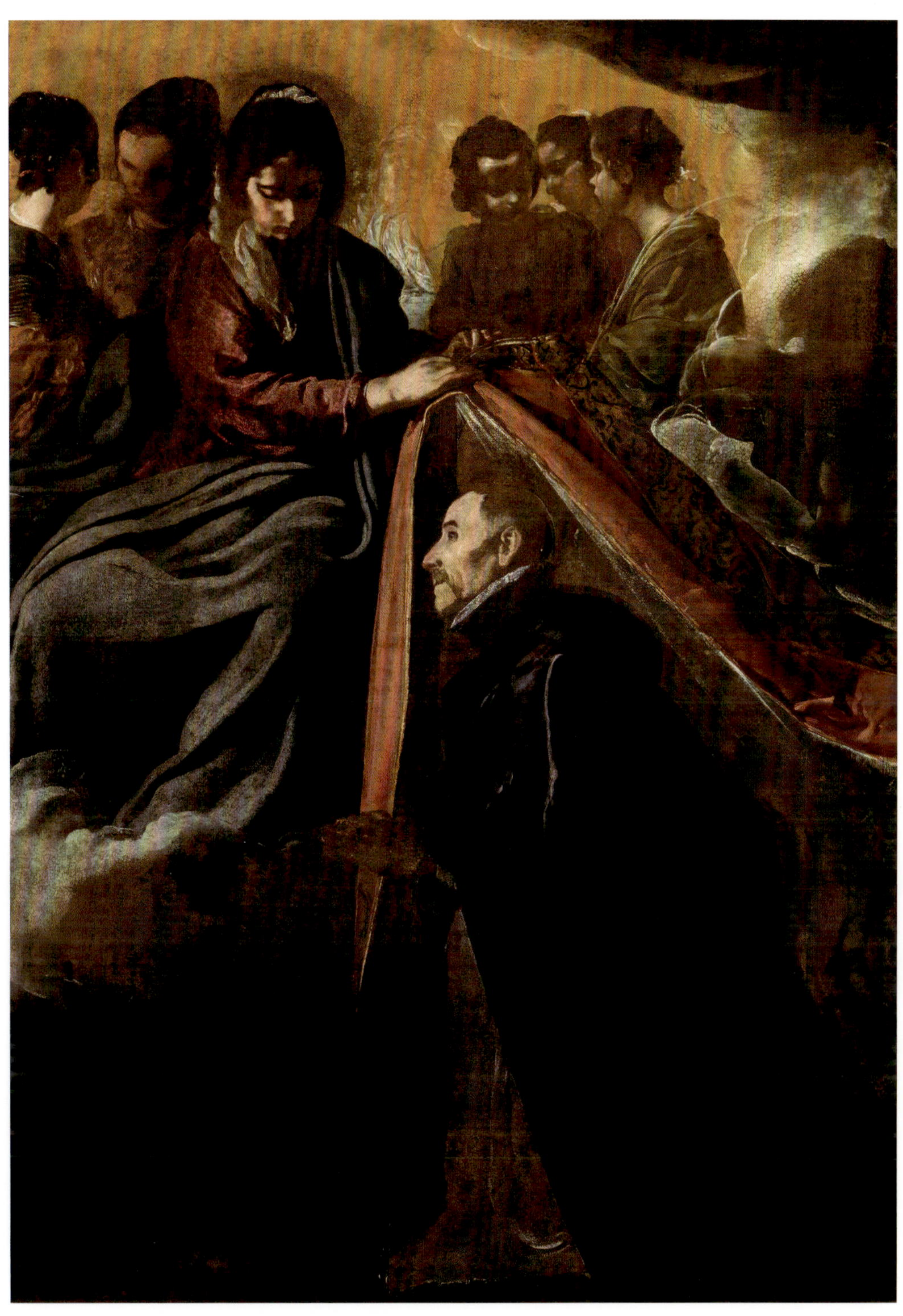

Pl. 4. Diego Velázquez, *Saint Ildefonso Receiving the Chasuble from the Virgin*, ca. 1622–23. Oil on canvas, 166 × 120 cm (65⅜ × 47¼ in.). Ayuntamiento de Sevilla

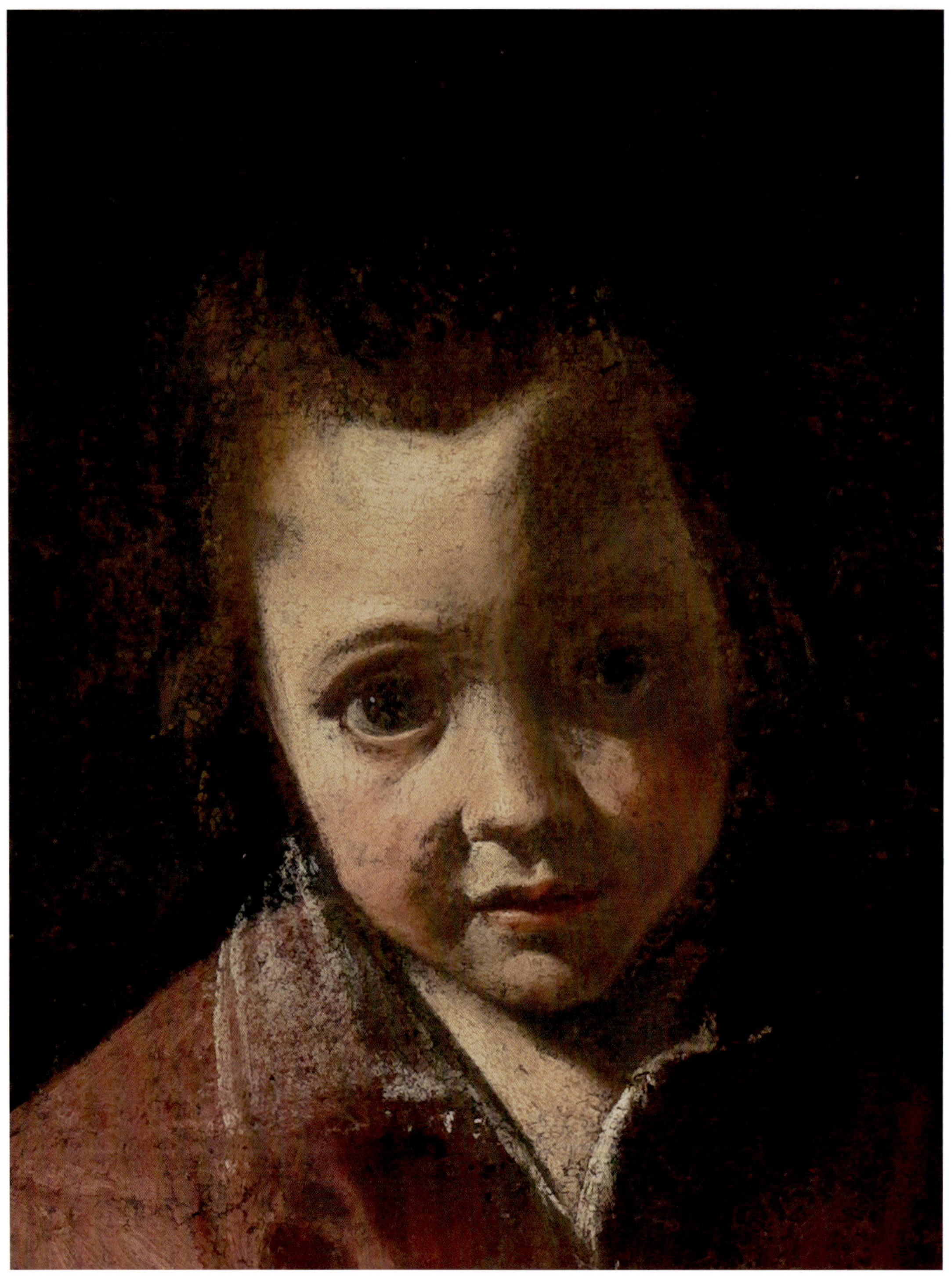

Diego Velázquez, detail of the *Education of the Virgin*, showing the head of the Virgin

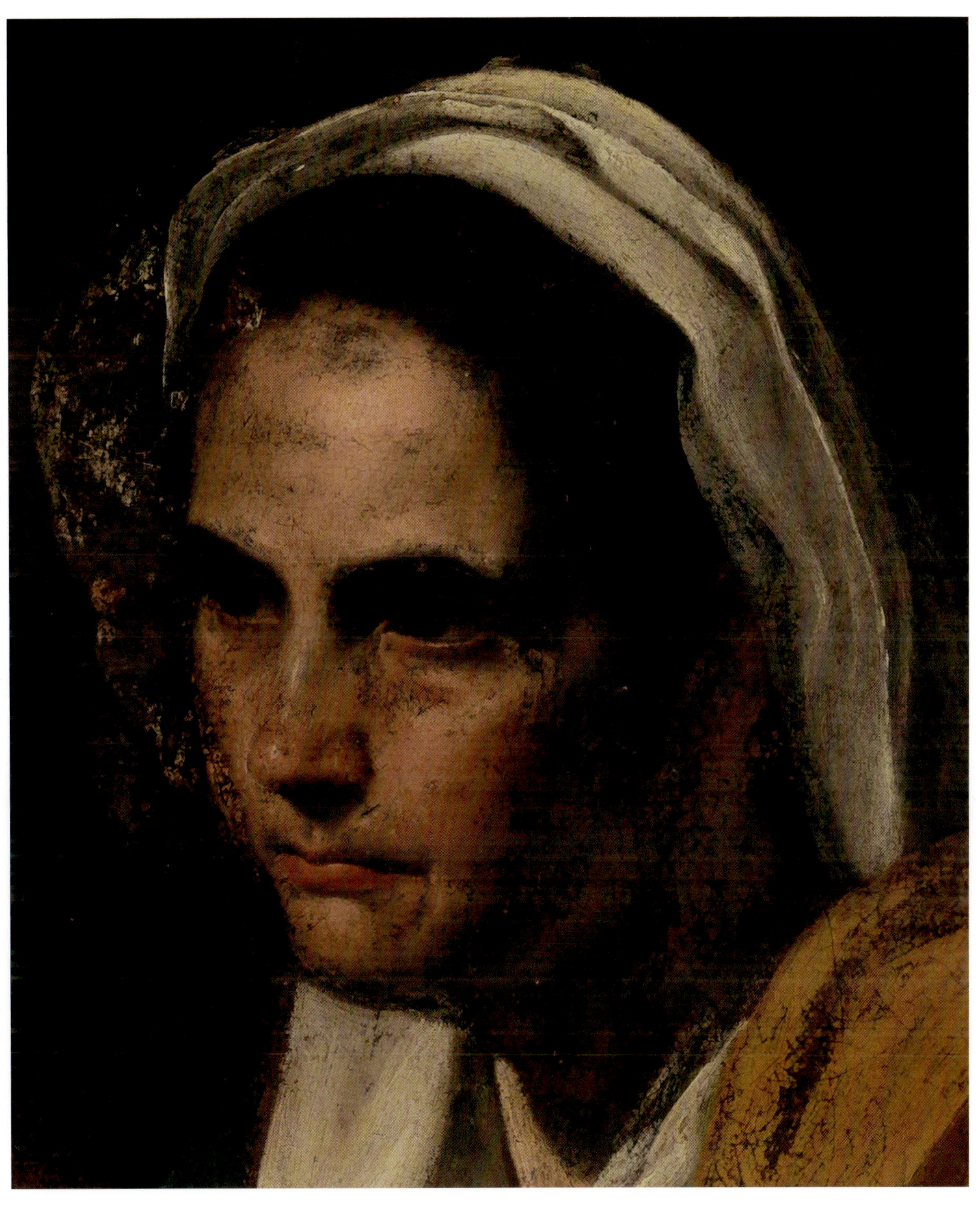

Diego Velázquez, detail of the *Education of the Virgin*, showing the head of Saint Anne

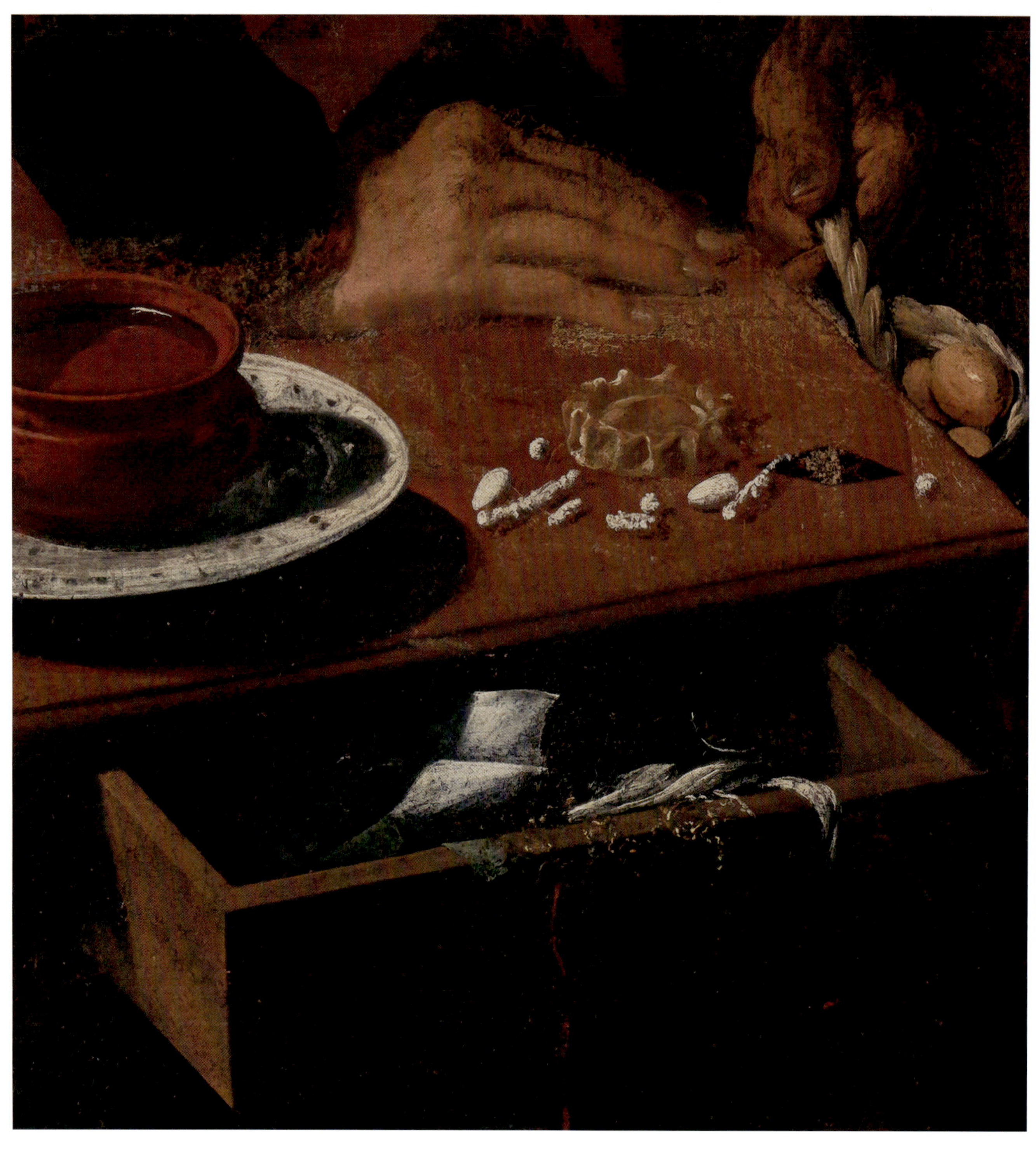

Diego Velázquez, detail of the *Education of the Virgin*, showing the low table at left with still-life elements

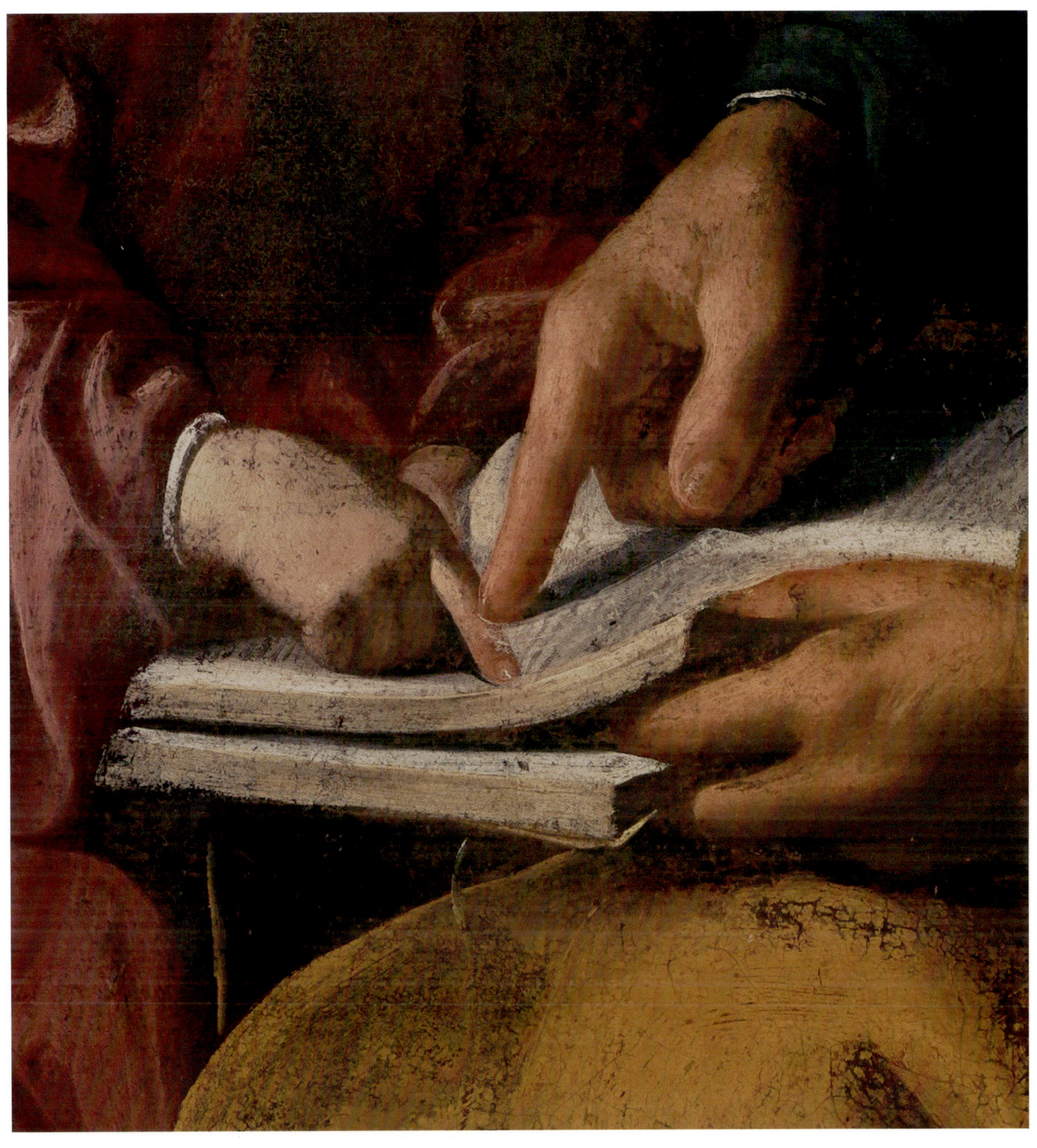

Diego Velázquez, detail of the *Education of the Virgin*, showing the fingers of the Virgin and Saint Anne pointing to the text

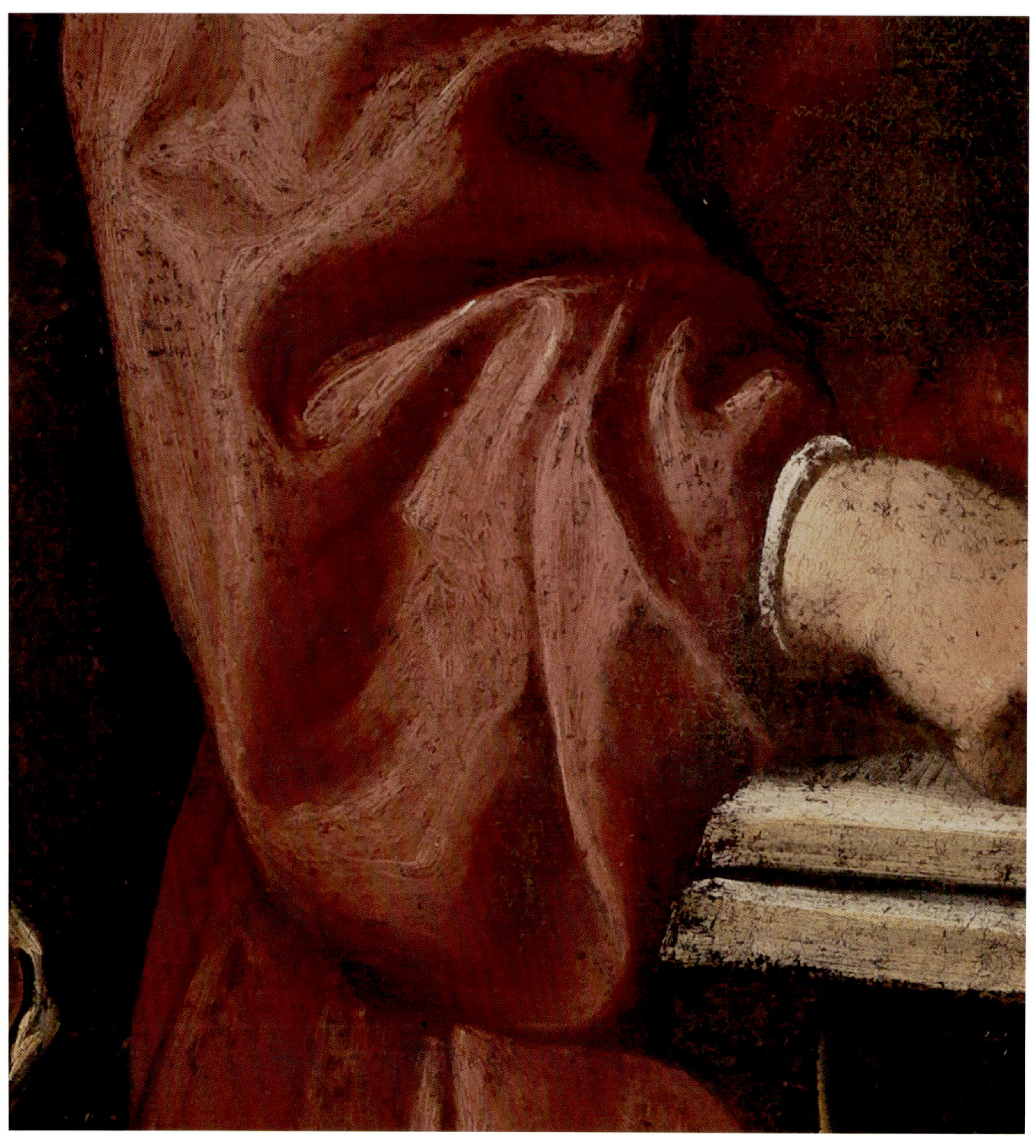

Diego Velázquez, detail of the *Education of the Virgin*, showing the sleeve of the Virgin

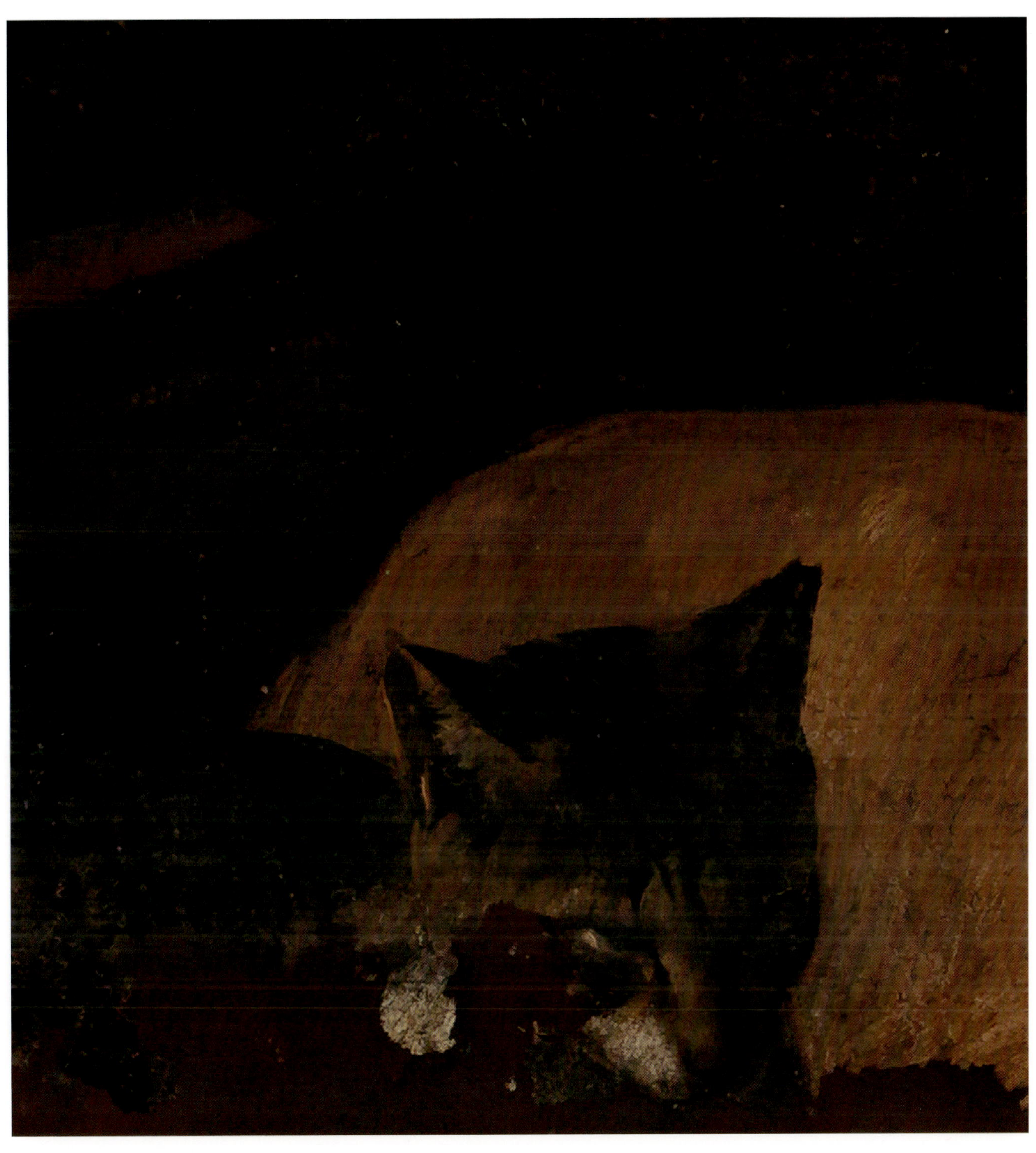

Diego Velázquez, detail of the *Education of the Virgin*, showing the cat at bottom left

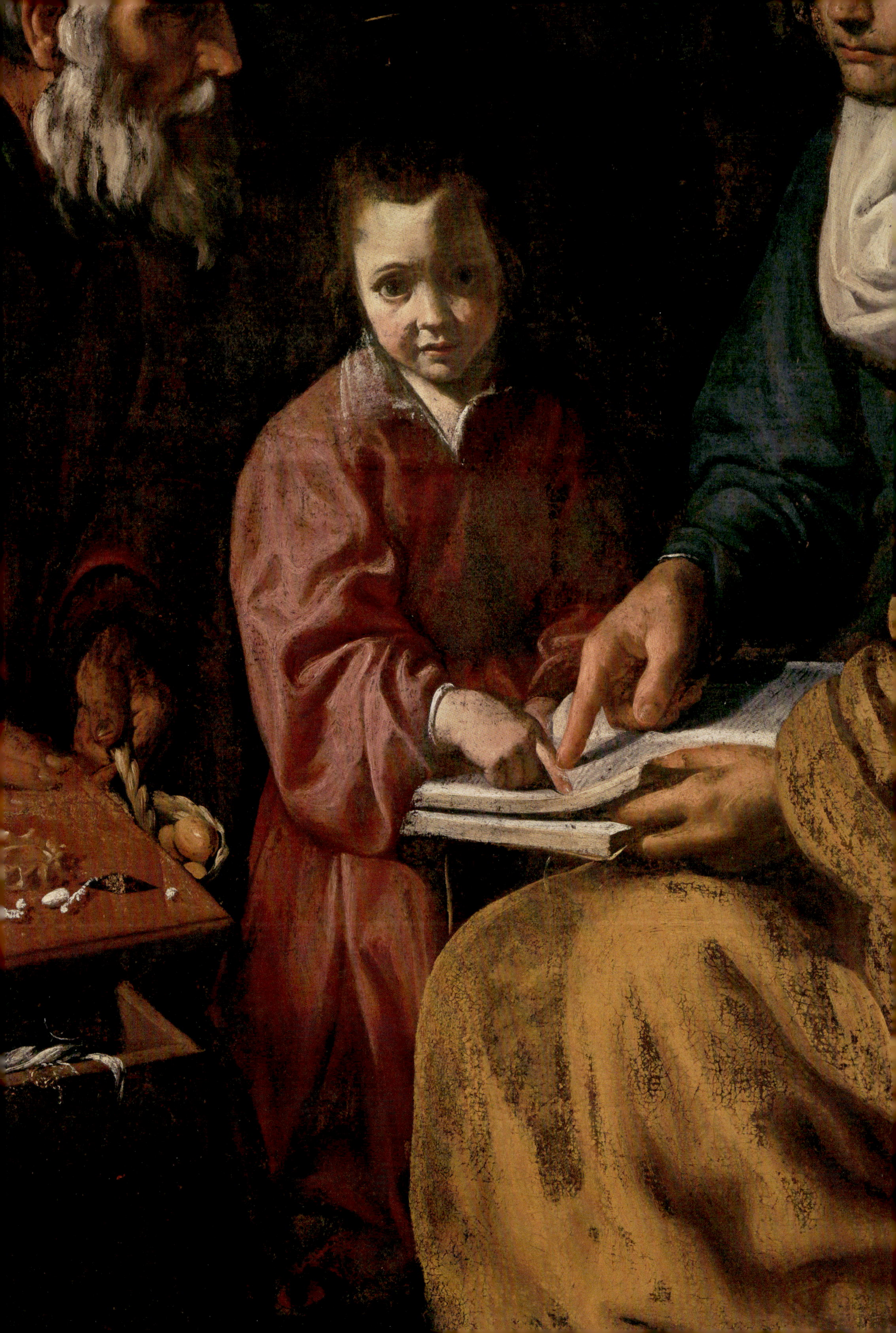

THE YOUNG VELÁZQUEZ

Yale's *Education of the Virgin*

JOHN MARCIARI

ny discussion of the *Education of the Virgin* at the Yale University Art Gallery (pl. 1) must begin by considering it alongside the work that was its clear inspiration, the painting of the same subject by Juan de Roelas (pl. 2). Painted for the Mercedarian convent in Seville around 1612, Roelas's altarpiece shows a teenaged Virgin Mary being taught to read by her mother, Saint Anne, who sits enthroned with a choir of angels in attendance. The cult of Saint Anne was long established in Seville, and there would be many Sevillian paintings and polychrome sculptures of the Education of the Virgin produced throughout the seventeenth century, but Roelas's painting seems to have been the city's first modern depiction of the subject. The painter and writer Francisco Pacheco, who had been Velázquez's master, introduced a discussion of the iconography in his *Arte de la pintura* (published posthumously in 1649 but compiled over many years before that) with the observation that:

> artists today depict the blessed Saint Anne teaching the Mother of God to read, a new subject, but one embraced by the vulgar. I say new, because it is about twenty-four years, more or less, from the time it began down to 1636, when a sculpture of Saint Anne in a chapel at the parochial church of the Magdalena was given by a modern sculptor an accompanying sculpture of the young Virgin reading.

Subtracting twenty-four years from 1636, one comes to 1612, the year in which Roelas's canvas seems to have been completed.[1] Although the reasons for Pacheco's elliptical language are unclear, Pacheco implies that Roelas's version was the earliest painting of the subject of which he was aware.[2]

The similarities between Roelas's canvas and the Yale painting are striking. In both compositions, the young Virgin Mary is at center, taught by a seated Saint Anne, with a dog, cat, and sewing basket in the foreground; scraps of fabric hang from the open drawer of the low table at the lower left of each picture, and atop those tables sit the same types of pastries and other sweetmeats. The Yale painting was long ago cut at the top, but enough remains of an angel in blue-green robes with clasped hands to understand that the upper part likewise resembled Roelas's model. So similar are the paintings that there can be no doubt that the Yale *Education* was painted in Seville by an artist with ready access to Roelas's work.

The differences between the two works, however, are perhaps more significant, particularly if we wish to understand the Yale painting. The addition of the Virgin's father, Joachim, is the most obvious change, but the substitution of a dark domestic interior, with humble furniture replacing the richly carved throne of Roelas's Saint Anne, is more dramatic. The Virgin in the Yale painting is a significantly younger girl, and she wears ordinary robes rather than the rich jewels, crown, and star- and pearl-covered drapery in Roelas's original. The facial expressions of the figures, and especially the young Virgin's direct outward gaze, confronting the eye of the viewer of the Yale canvas, also mark an important reinterpretation of the subject.

The crux of these differences is a fundamentally changed approach to naturalism, and that change represents a generational, if not an epochal, shift in the art of painting. If one looks for other examples of that revolutionary change in the art of Seville in the early years of the seventeenth century, they can be found, essentially, only in the work of one painter: the young Diego Velázquez.

Countless parallels exist between the Yale *Education* and other works by the young artist. The mise-en-scène recalls that of the *Tavern Scene* at the Hermitage (fig. 1), not only in the shadowy interior but also in the way in which the figures sit uneasily in their space, treated not entirely consistently but rather as individually studied elements with resulting disruptions of scale and perspective.[3] The same can be said, too, of the *Two Young Men at a Table* at Apsley House, in London (fig. 2), the *Old Woman Cooking Eggs* at the National Galleries of Scotland (fig. 3), and the *Supper at Emmaus* at the Metropolitan Museum of Art (fig. 4).[4] These paintings likewise contain a common mix of still-life elements: the red clay bowl at left in the Yale *Education*, the blue-and-white plate beneath it, and the short-handled basket held by Saint Joachim are akin to objects seen in these other paintings, and also in works like the *Kitchen Maid* at the Art Institute of Chicago (fig. 5) or the *Kitchen Scene with Christ in the House of Martha and Mary* at the National Gallery, London (fig. 6). Just as the young artist tended to carry similar objects from one composition to the next, so too he was consistent in the drapery that constitutes the garments worn by his figures, gathered in heavy folds with highlights drawn in long, curving strokes of paint.

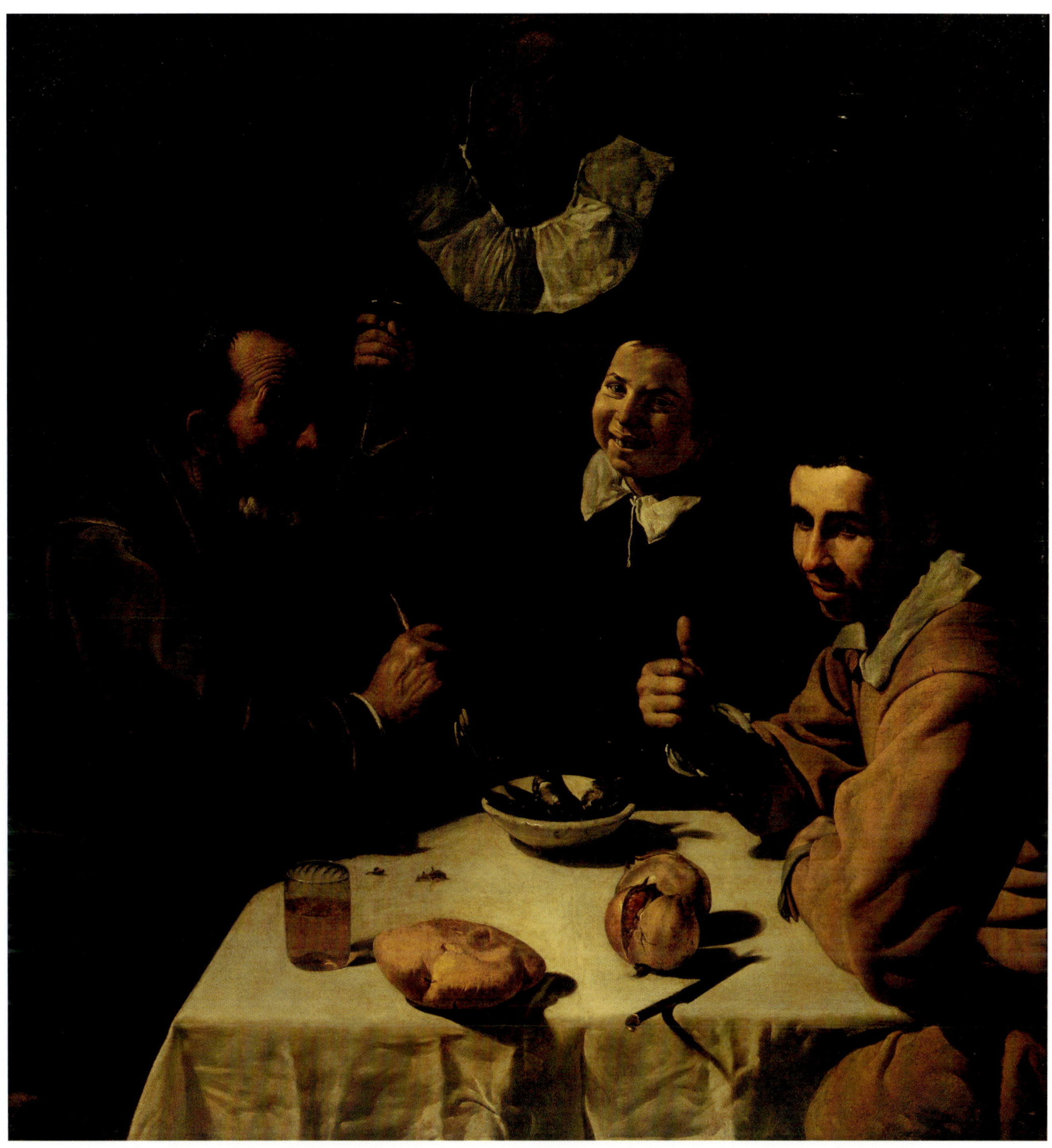

Fig. 1. Diego Velázquez, *Tavern Scene*, ca. 1616–17. Oil on canvas, 108.5 × 102 cm (42¾ × 40³⁄₁₆ in.). State Hermitage Museum, Saint Petersburg, inv. no. 389

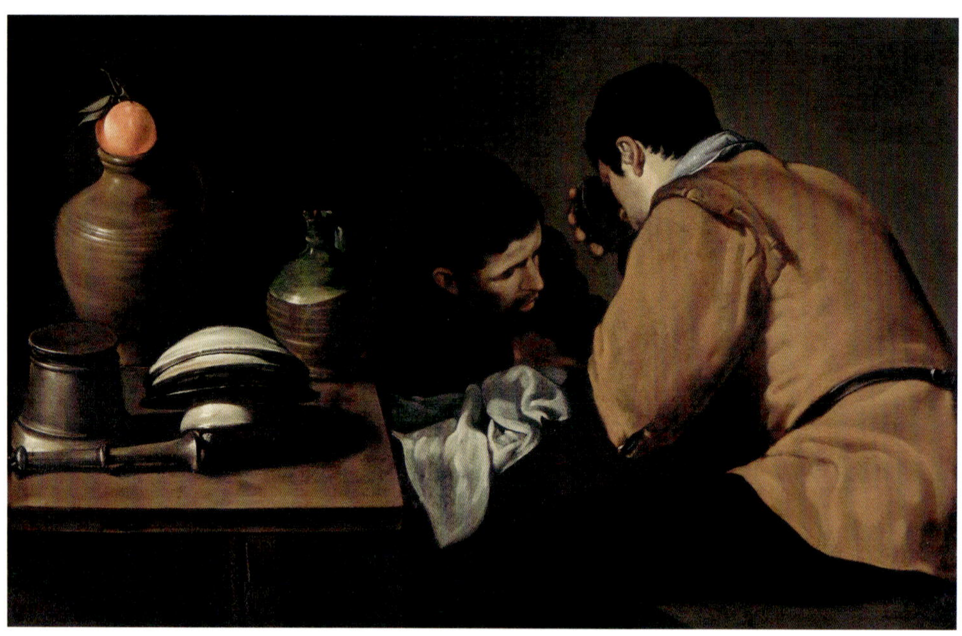

Fig. 2. Diego Velázquez, *Two Young Men at a Table*, ca. 1618. Oil on canvas, 65 × 104 cm (25⅝ × 40¹⁵⁄₁₆ in.). Wellington Collection, Apsley House, London

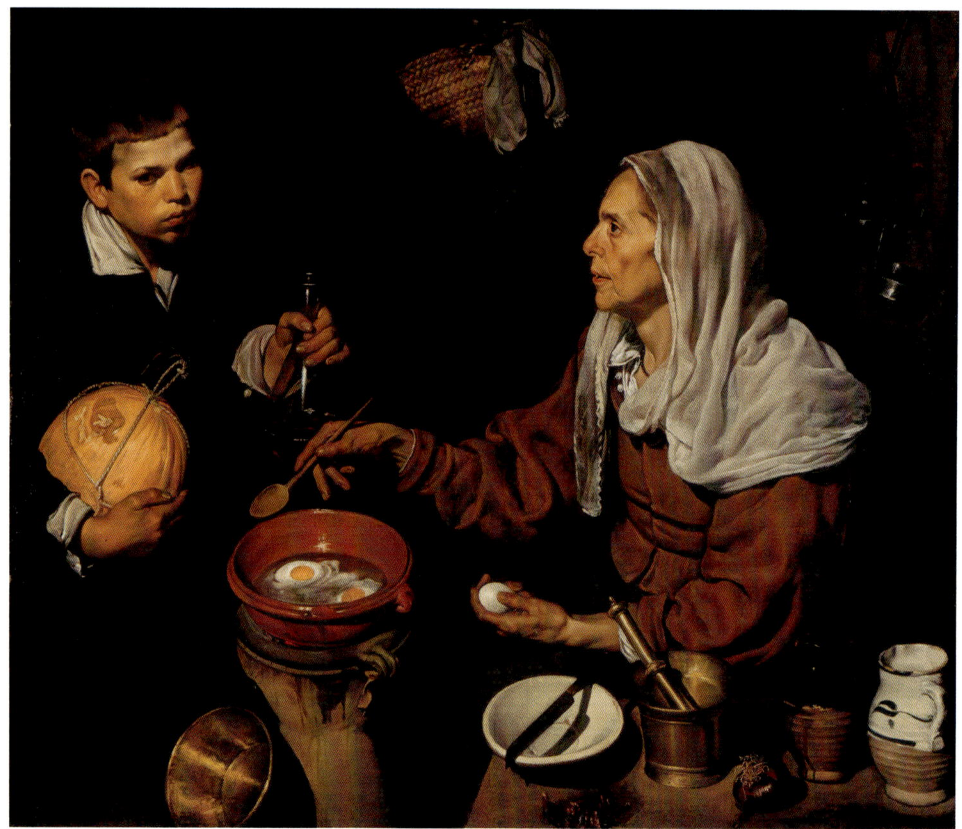

Fig. 3. Diego Velázquez, *An Old Woman Cooking Eggs*, 1618. Oil on canvas, 101 × 120 cm (39¾ × 47¼ in.). National Galleries of Scotland, Edinburgh, Purchased with the aid of the Art Fund, 1955, inv. no. NG2180

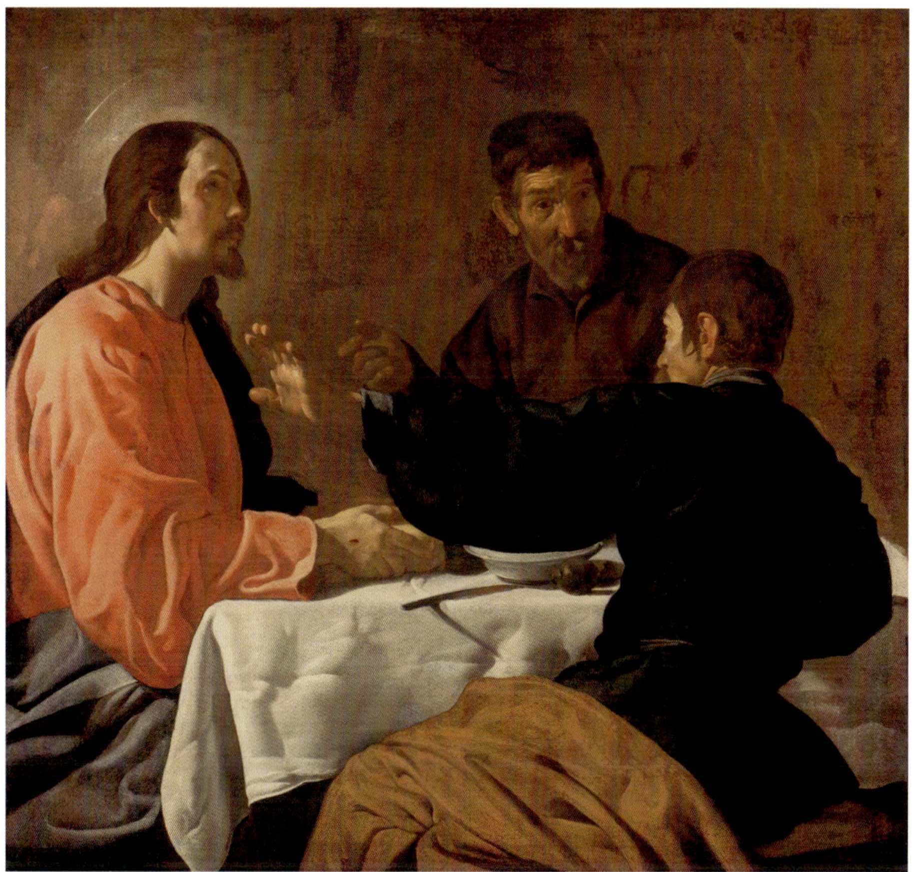

Fig. 4. Diego Velázquez, *The Supper at Emmaus*, ca. 1622. Oil on canvas, 123 × 133 cm (48⁷⁄₁₆ × 52³⁄₈ in.). Metropolitan Museum of Art, New York, Bequest of Benjamin Altman, 1913, inv. no. 14.40.631

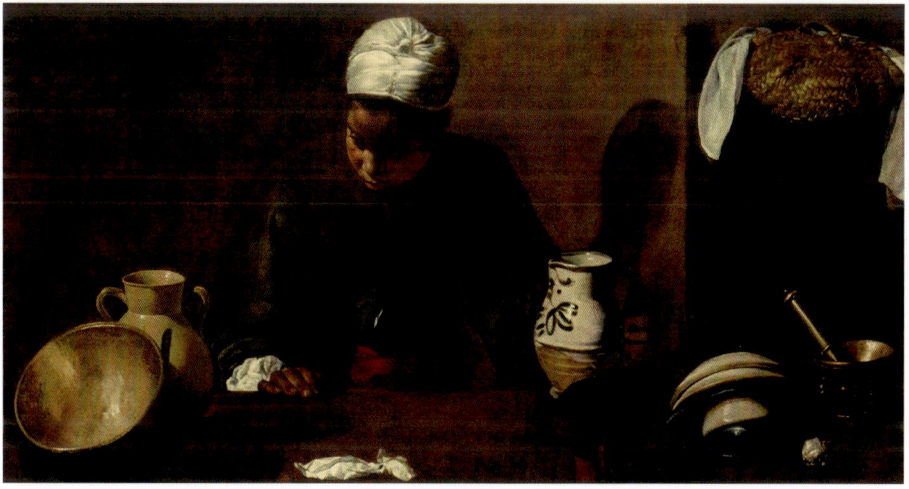

Fig. 5. Diego Velázquez, *A Kitchen Maid*, ca. 1618. Oil on canvas, 56 × 104 cm (22¹⁄₁₆ × 40¹⁵⁄₁₆ in.). Art Institute of Chicago, Robert Waller Memorial Fund, inv. no. 1935.380

The prominent ochre drapery worn by Saint Anne, for example, is especially close to that worn by Saint Thomas in the painting at the Musée des Beaux-Arts d'Orléans (fig. 7), and the draperies of the young Virgin bear close comparison to those worn by the Virgin in the *Immaculate Conception* at the National Gallery, London (fig. 8), even if the rose-colored garment in the Yale painting does not shimmer with the celestial light of the London scene. For a young artist so intent on realism, Velázquez is likely to have studied the same studio props, and perhaps even the same heavy pieces of cloth, as he worked on painting after painting. It is hardly surprising, then, to see him also evidently employing the same studio models for multiple works, such that the young woman serving as the Virgin in the London *Immaculate Conception* reprises her role in the Prado's *Adoration of the Magi*, and the same old man seems to have served as a model for the Yale *Education*, the Hermitage *Tavern Scene*, and the *Saint Paul* at the Museu Nacional d'Art de Catalunya, Barcelona.[5] What is more, the manner in which these men are painted is remarkably consistent. Looking at the wrinkled brow of the old men in the Yale and Hermitage paintings, for example, we find the gathered flesh delineated with high contours of thick paint, a technical feature that has been noted elsewhere as characteristic of the young Velázquez.[6] On the basis of these comparisons alone, it would be

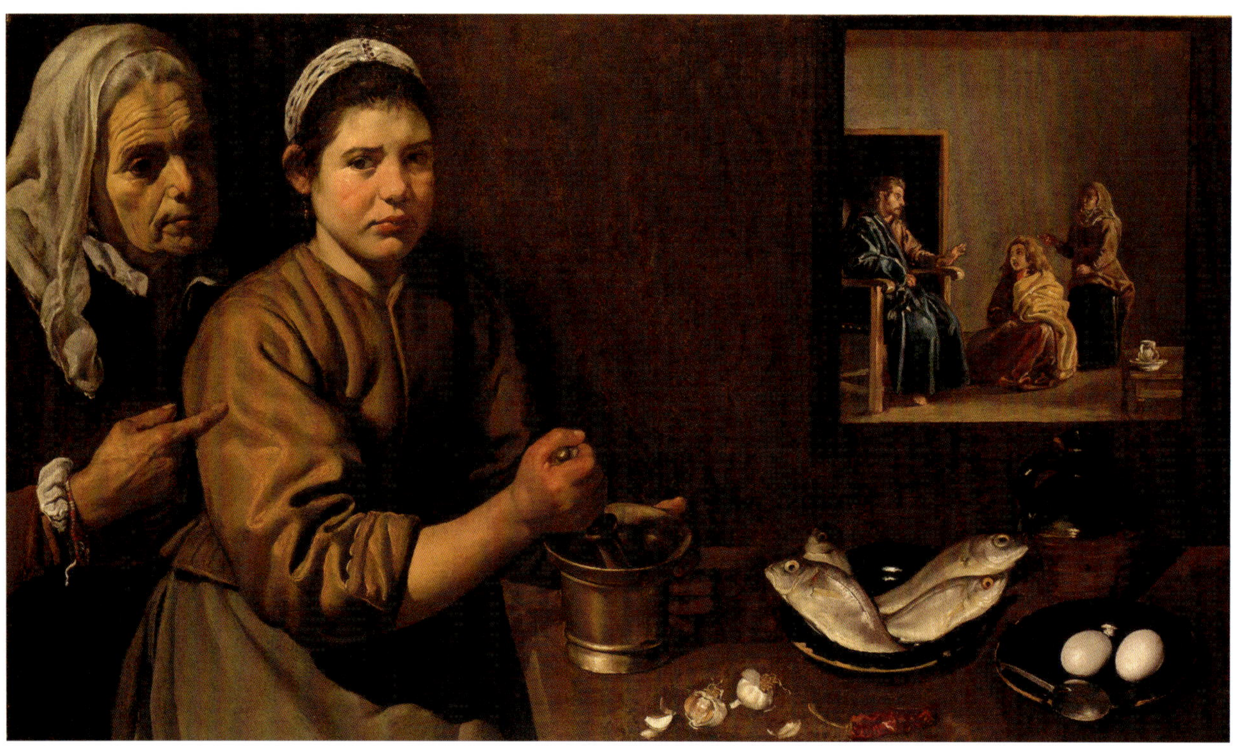

Fig. 6. Diego Velázquez, *Kitchen Scene with Christ in the House of Martha and Mary*, 1618. Oil on canvas, 60 × 104 cm (23⅝ × 40¹⁵⁄₁₆ in.). National Gallery, London, inv. no. NG 1375

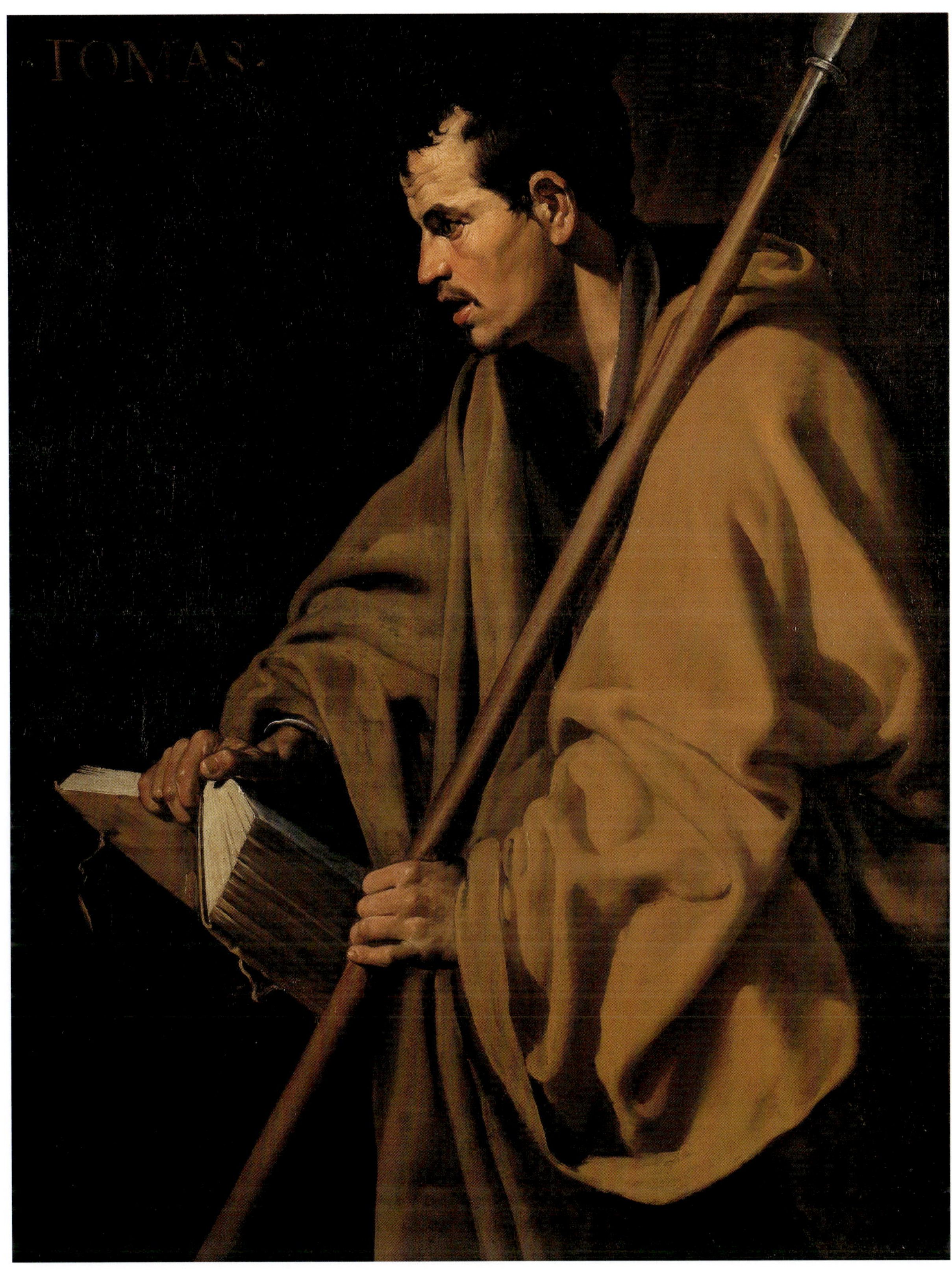

Fig. 7. Diego Velázquez, *Saint Thomas*, ca. 1619. Oil on canvas, 105 × 85 cm (41⅜ × 33½ in.). Musée des Beaux-Arts d'Orléans, inv. no. 1556A

difficult to argue convincingly that the Yale painting is by anyone other than Velázquez.

Beyond the matter of common elements and similar style, however, important conceptual differences between Roelas's *Education* and the Yale painting likewise point to Velázquez as the creator of the latter. Some of these differences can be explained with reference to Pacheco's thoughts on Roelas's painting, for even if Pacheco's *Arte de la pintura* was not published until long after the Yale painting would have been made, Pacheco's opinion of Roelas's work was probably formed—and shared with his pupils and assistants—shortly after that painting was completed. In his long discussion of the iconography of the Education of the Virgin, Pacheco notes that Roelas was lacking in decorum and explains that the Virgin in Roelas's painting, who appeared to him to be thirteen or fourteen years old, would not have needed to learn how to read. Holding fast to the doctrine of the Immaculate Conception, so important in seventeenth-century Spain, Pacheco explains that the Virgin was born with perfect use of reason, free will, and contemplation and need not have received such instruction. Yet, Pacheco acknowledges that just as Christ, as an example of humility and to honor his parents, learned the skills of carpentry in Joseph's workshop, so too the Virgin may have followed her mother's lesson, such that it was not entirely inappropriate to depict her as a pupil.[7]

The Yale painting seems deliberately intended to correct the errors that Pacheco perceived in Roelas's work. The Virgin is a much younger girl, more appropriate in the role of student.[8] More importantly, though, the Virgin stares directly outward from the center of the scene. In meeting our eye, she seems to acknowledge that she is merely play-acting, *pretending* to learn how to read. This is a Virgin of the Immaculate Conception variety, all-knowing and preternaturally wise, somewhat to the befuddlement of her onlooking parents. In meeting our gaze, the Virgin makes viewers of the painting into something like complicit spectators, accomplices in the pageant of filial piety. The composition is a brilliantly sophisticated solution to the problems that Pacheco perceived in Roelas's painting of the subject.

Even if based on Roelas's work and addressing Pacheco's criticisms, the Yale painting signals a new way of thinking about the representation of sacred history. Its naturalism challenges the previous generation's practice of idealization. More significantly, there is a self-consciousness about the act of making and looking at pictures that is implicit in the very conception of the Yale canvas. Such self-consciousness, based on sophisticated understanding of both the subject of the painting and of the art of painting itself, has long been identified as one of the hallmarks of Velázquez's work. It is of course most clearly seen in late masterpieces such as the Prado's *Las meninas*, but the same mind—the same pictorial intelligence—is already palpable in the Yale canvas. This essential quality of

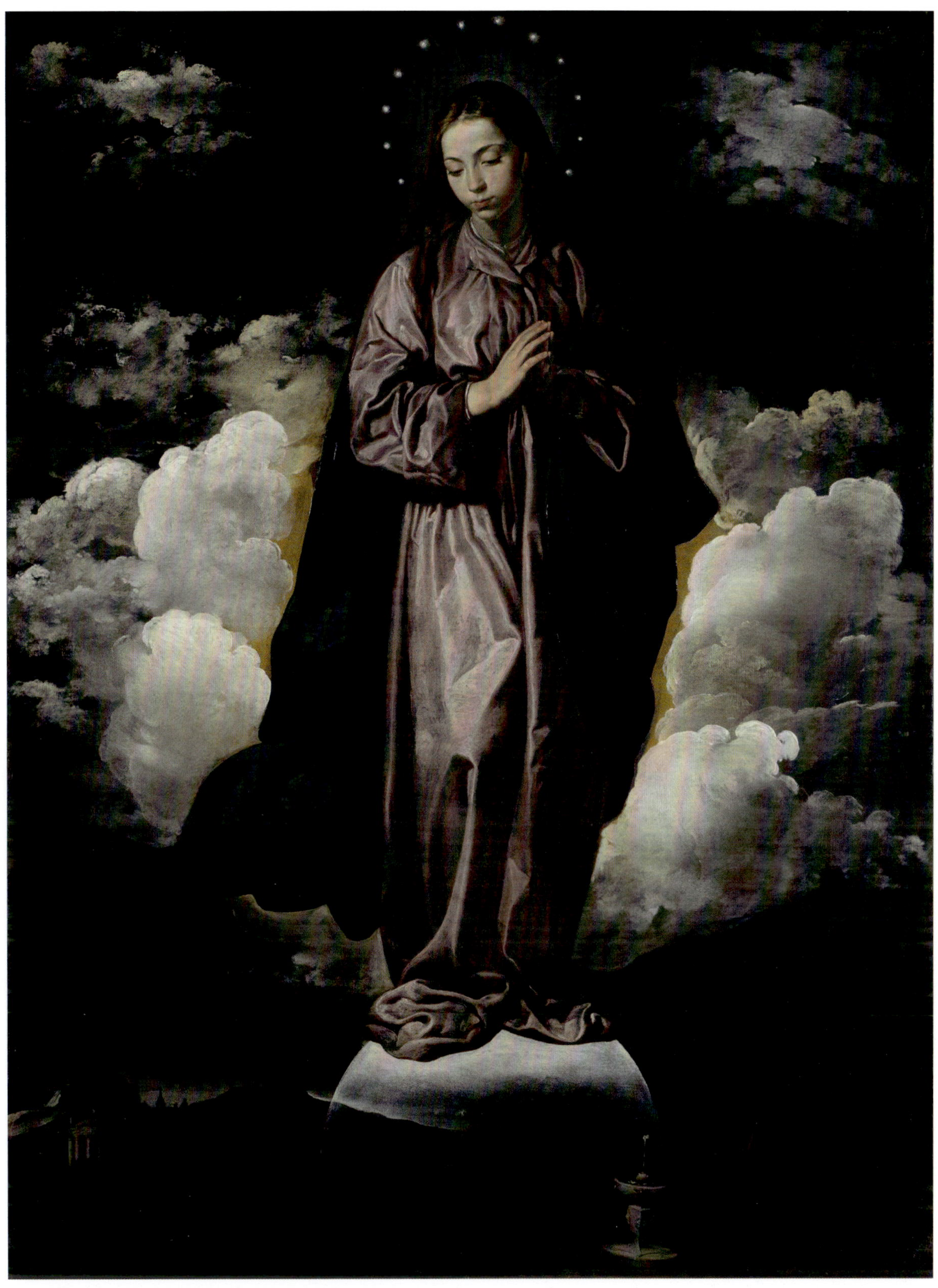

Fig. 8. Diego Velázquez, *The Immaculate Conception*, 1618–19. Oil on canvas, 135 ×
102 cm (53³⁄₁₆ × 40³⁄₁₆ in.). National Gallery, London, Bought with the aid of the
Art Fund, 1974, inv. no. NG 6424

Velázquez's early work has recently been evocatively described by Lorenzo Pericolo, who notes of the Metropolitan Museum's *Supper at Emmaus* that the figures "seal the picture's fictiveness by entering the beholder's spatial field and mixing the inner and outer spaces of the representation."[9]

It is impossible to connect the Yale painting to any other known artist of early seventeenth-century Seville, but conversely, the intelligence of the painting argues against the possibility that this canvas is by some *pasticheur*, some unknown follower of Velázquez, as has been suggested by Jonathan Brown and others.[10] One might admit that there are clumsy passages in the Yale painting and an inconsistent handling of space. Such flaws are hardly surprising if one believes this to be the work of a very young painter barely out of his master's studio, for Velázquez would have been only eighteen or nineteen years old when he painted it. Yet, these perspectival inconsistencies also result from a revolutionary manner of composing works as a collage of objects studied from life. One finds the same qualities in the early paintings of Caravaggio and his followers in Rome, and, as has also been noted of those works, this new approach to painting seems deliberately to accept such disconnections, which draw attention to the act of painting.[11]

Furthermore, the recent conservation campaign has revealed that the artist labored over the Yale painting, working and reworking the composition.[12] These changes represent a fury of invention that is somewhat inexplicable in a pastiche. This canvas is a world away from those that merely copy Velázquez's paintings, or those that combine his motifs into new compositions: for example, the lifeless *Tavern Scene* in the Szépmüvészeti Múzeum, Budapest, which substitutes the two youths of the Hermitage *Tavern Scene* with new figures.[13] It seems wholly unlikely, moreover, that an artist looking to profit by working in imitation of Velázquez would have chosen to copy a painting by Roelas and to paint it in Velázquez's style. It is even more improbable that some otherwise unknown minor artist would have done so while channeling not only stylistic motifs but also Velázquez's forceful pictorial intelligence.

It has also been suggested that the young Velázquez would not have based a work on a painting by Roelas, the great rival of Velázquez's master, Pacheco.[14] On the one hand, the patrons of the Yale canvas—most likely the Carmelite nuns at the convent of Santa Ana, as will be discussed—may well have requested a work akin to the one by Roelas, who was himself a Carmelite friar, leaving the young Velázquez with relatively little choice about the expected composition. On the other hand, if one accepts that Pacheco and Roelas were heads of rival camps of painters, it seems entirely plausible that Velázquez would paint a canvas that corrected the errors that Pacheco perceived in the work of his rival.

Putting aside the rivalry of Pacheco and Roelas, Sevillian artists of the time often based new works on earlier compositions. Thus, for example, when in 1589 Pacheco took up a commission to paint a *Christ Carrying the Cross*, he essentially reproduced a mural of around 1561 that Luis de Vargas had painted on the exterior of the cathedral. The young Velázquez followed this pattern. His 1619 *Adoration of the Magi* is based on Alejo Fernández's painting of 1509–12 in the cathedral,[15] and his *Saint John the Evangelist* in London derives from an engraving by Jan Sadeler.[16] Sometimes, the adoption was less of an entire composition than of a remarkable motif, as in the case with the window conceit in Velázquez's *Martha and Mary*, which is drawn from Pacheco's *Saint Sebastian Attended by Saint Irene* of 1616. Velázquez's *Saint Ildefonso Receiving the Chasuble* (pl. 4), like the *Education of the Virgin* a relatively new subject when painted by the artist, also relied on a recently completed model: a lost altarpiece alternately attributed to Juan de Uceda or to Juan de Roelas.[17]

The Yale *Education of the Virgin* is a juvenile work, seemingly painted around 1617–18 and thus among the earliest known paintings by Velázquez. The work builds on the tradition of Sevillian art of the early seventeenth century. Despite its flaws, however, the work points to the greatness that Velázquez alone among his Sevillian contemporaries would achieve.

While Velázquez's training in the academy of Francisco Pacheco can explain some of the elements of the Yale painting, Pacheco's own paintings give virtually no precedent for Velázquez's naturalism and style, and one wonders how the young artist could have so far surpassed his master.[18] Discussions in Pacheco's academy surely inspired the young artist to ask himself questions about the essential nature of art. This alone can partly explain Velázquez's break with the traditions of Sevillian painting. One wonders, nonetheless, where Velázquez might have found precedents or inspiration for the radical naturalism typical of his work but entirely absent from Pacheco's. The polychrome sculpture of Seville was surely one such source, readily at hand not only because of the strong local tradition but also because Pacheco was responsible for painting the surfaces of sculpture by major masters such as Juan Martínez Montañés.[19] In its breaking of the barriers between the spectator and the work of art, the palpably real painted sculpture of Seville could thus have served as a starting point for Velázquez, just as the sculptures at the North Italian *sacri monti* seem to have inspired Lombard naturalist painters, including Caravaggio.

A second set of works may also have been a key model for Velázquez: the paintings in the city of Toledo, where the traditions of Caravaggio's naturalism were first fully visible in Spain. Velázquez's naturalism is often linked to Caravaggio's example, although there has been surprisingly little concrete discussion of where the young Velázquez may have seen Caravaggesque paintings.[20] Velázquez is not documented as being in Toledo as a young man, but it is hardly implausible to suggest that he may have accompanied Pacheco on a trip north. Pacheco was in Toledo in 1611, although this would have been too early for the trip to have meant much to a still very young Velázquez if he had accompanied his master.[21] We must hypothesize that Velázquez returned a few years later, perhaps encouraged to do so by Pacheco, whose own travels left a lasting impression on his art. Such a trip would explain much, for while there was no realist tradition in Sevillian painting, Toledo was another matter entirely. By 1611 Juan Bautista Maíno had returned from his trip to Italy, where he had spent time in Rome at the height of *caravaggismo*; he was soon afterward working on the *retablo mayor* of the church of San Pedro Mártir in Toledo, perhaps the first major monument of Caravaggesque naturalism in Spain (fig. 9).[22] The impact of a trip to Italy, and also of Maíno's new paintings, can also be seen in the work of another local master in Toledo, Luis Tristán, who, after a trip to Rome, departed from the early manner that he had learned in the studio of El Greco; by the mid-1610s, Tristán was already creating works like the *Holy Family* in the Minneapolis Institute of Arts (pl. 3), the similarity of which to Velázquez's *Education of the Virgin* is evident.[23] By the mid-1610s, a number of native Italian painters and paintings were also present in Toledo and offered access to the new naturalist tradition. Maíno's work is often compared, for

example, to that of Carlo Saraceni, whom he probably knew in Rome; Saraceni would himself send three canvases to the cathedral in Toledo in 1613–14.[24]

In time, Caravaggesque pictures would make their way to Seville as well, for example, in the collection of the duke of Alcalá at the Casa de Pilatos, although that collection arrived from Italy only in the late 1620s.[25] The *Crucifixion of Saint Peter* at the church of San Alberto in Seville is also based on Caravaggio's painting of the subject, although the date of the Sevillian version is not known.[26] When the young Velázquez came of age, however, the critical mass of Italian Baroque naturalism in Spain was in Toledo. Any of the works mentioned above could have signaled the path that Velázquez might follow, but to have seen all of them together must have constituted a dramatic eye-opening experience for the young man from Seville.

Extreme naturalism potentially undermined the depiction of sacred themes, drawing attention to the act of painting as much as to the thing being depicted. Pacheco and his contemporaries, the artists and theorists of the older generation, must have seen such pictorial strategies as powerful but confrontational, even subversive, when employed in sacred painting. Just as Federico Zuccaro and the older generation of Roman painters had maligned Caravaggio's work, so too Vicente Carducho in Spain fought against *caravaggismo*.[27] The young Velázquez, however, eagerly employed the new style. In his *Arte de la pintura*, Pacheco praises Velázquez's *bodegones*

(genre scenes) and portraits, but he makes
no mention of any of Velázquez's sacred
paintings done in Seville (nor does he
mention the similarly conceived altarpiec-
es by Zurbarán). This silence is puzzling,
but a work like the *Education of the Virgin*
would have presented a direct challenge to
Pacheco's own elevated, idealized treatment
of sacred themes. Was Pacheco's omission
of such works a means of avoiding the
critique of the first works by his greatest pupil (and son-in-law), who had also
become the painter to the king by the time
that the *Arte de la pintura* was published?
Might Pacheco's notably strict analysis of
Roelas's *Education of the Virgin* have also
been a veiled criticism about Velázquez's
own early religious paintings?

Returning to the matter of Velázquez's
youth, we might consider the question of the
commission for the *Education of the Virgin*.
The work is entirely undocumented, though
this is the case for virtually all of Velázquez's
Sevillian paintings, and none of his early
religious works is recorded before the late
eighteenth century. The Education of the
Virgin is a subject connected to the cult of
Saint Anne in Seville, but it seems highly unlikely that the principal Sevillian church dedicated to the saint, the rich church of Santa
Ana de Triana, would have commissioned an
altarpiece from an unknown teenager barely
removed from his master's studio.

    The Carmelite convent of Santa Ana,
however, may well have been the original location of the painting. The convent
was founded in Paterna del Campo in

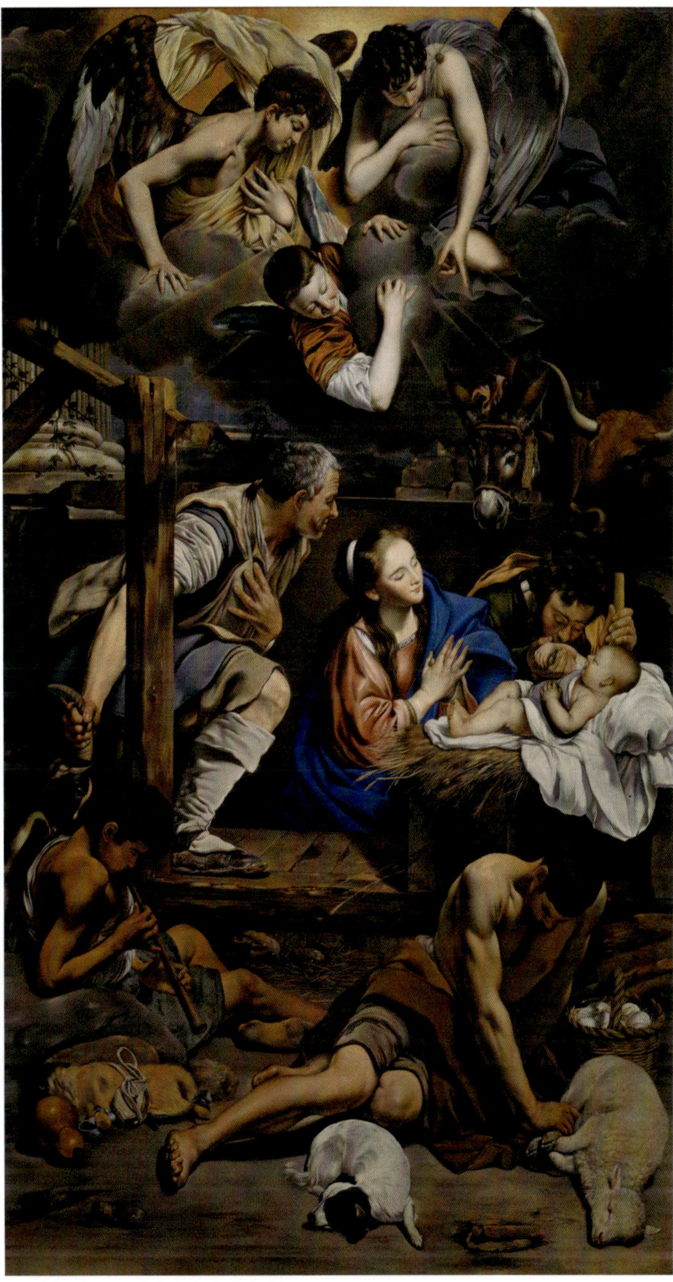

Fig. 9. Juan Bautista Maíno, *The Adoration of the
Shepherds*, from the *retablo mayor* of the church of
San Pedro Mártir, 1612–14. Oil on canvas, 315 ×
174 cm (10 ft. 4¹⁄₁₆ in. × 68½ in.). Museo Nacional
del Prado, Madrid, inv. no. P-3227

1537 and moved to Seville in 1594 but was transferred to its current location near the Alameda only in 1606. The sculpted retable over the high altar today was brought to the church from the convent of Belén when the two Carmelite houses merged in 1746. The high altar was previously decorated, significantly, with the sculptural *Education of the Virgin* group by Martínez Montañés that is now at the upper center of the retable. The Martínez Montañés group dates to around 1627 and was probably commissioned following damage to the church in the flood of 1626, a flood so severe that it required the nuns of the convent to take shelter in the choir loft.[28] There is no record of the church decoration prior to this time; nor is there any earlier painting or sculpture in the church today. Given the subject matter and Velázquez's record of working for the Carmelites,[29] the Yale painting may well have served as the altarpiece before the flood. If removed from the main body of the church after 1626, the lack of subsequent influence, copies, or documentary record might also thus be explained. The canvas could have then been kept, inaccessible, somewhere in the convent until the nineteenth-century deconsecrations that provided early collectors with many opportunities to purchase Sevillian paintings. Writing in 1817, Ceán Bermúdez refers to many paintings being sent at the time to England, "where they [were] stacked away and totally despised" and to merchants moving from Seville to London "loaded with paintings of the Sevillian school, which were claimed in England to be by Murillo and other Andalusian painters."[30] This wholesale exporting of paintings from Spain to England continued throughout the first half of the nineteenth century, and it is easy to imagine that the damaged *Education of the Virgin* could have been one such work, carried to England without a secure attribution or any record of its provenance.

Having presumably left Spain in the first half of the nineteenth century, the canvas arrived at Yale about a generation later. Its accession number at Yale (1900.43) would normally indicate that the picture arrived in 1900, but this is misleading, for that number was assigned in 1959, when an inventory of the collection turned up a number of works that had never been formally accessioned; those for which the provenance was then unknown were given inventory numbers beginning with 1900. Appended to the minutes of the Gallery's Governing Board meeting for 1946, however, is the transcription of a memo from the Yale School of the Fine Arts' records of 1925, which recorded the gift from Henry Hotchkiss Townshend and his brother, Raynham Townshend, of "two paintings, oil on canvas, framed, Spanish, style of Murillo, religious subjects." There are no other paintings that were then in the Gallery's collection that could fit this description. Moreover, the earliest studio photographs of the *Education of the Virgin* date to 1946, likewise supporting the argument that the painting was that with which

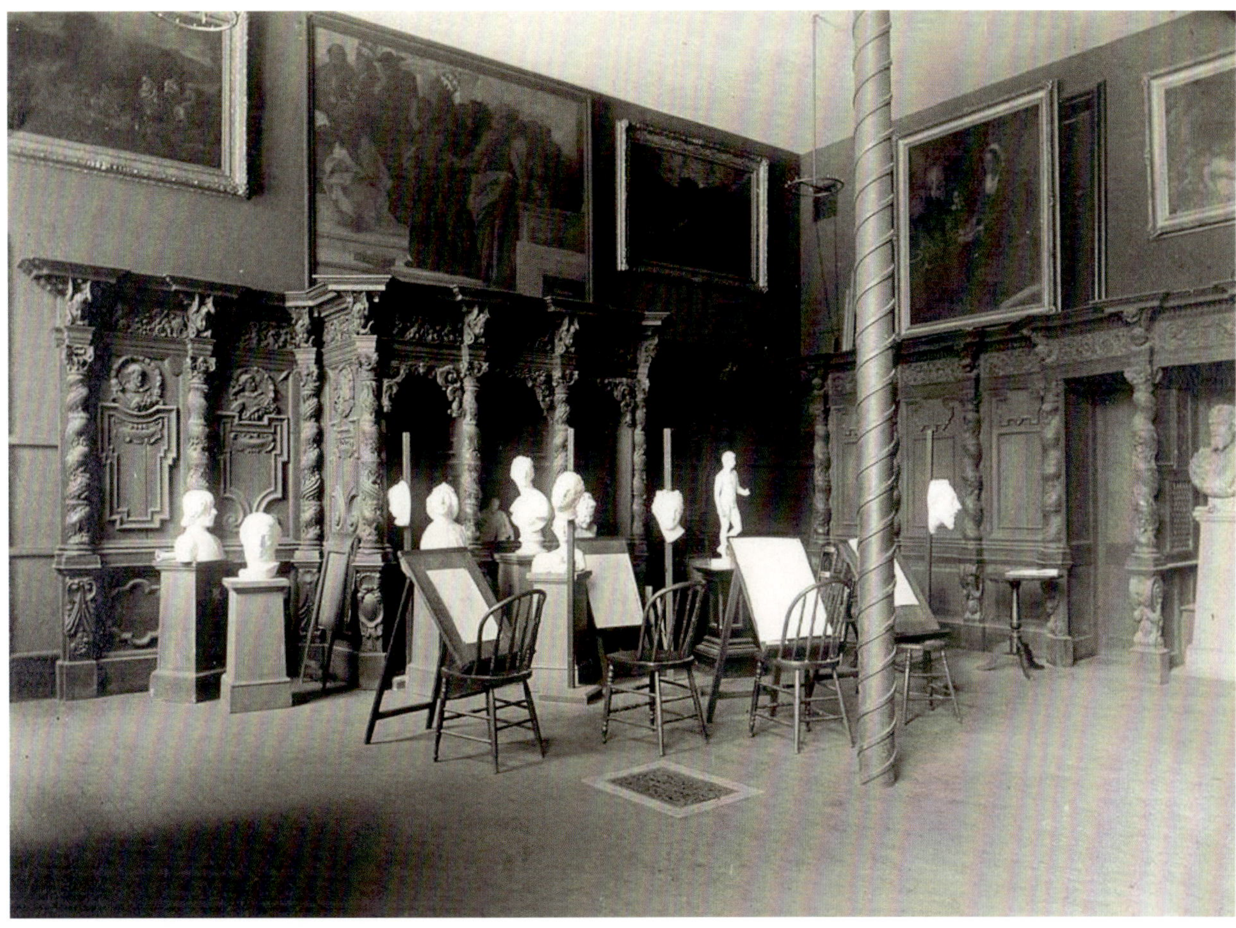

Fig. 10. *The Education of the Virgin*, in situ at top right at the Yale School of the
Fine Arts, Street Hall, New Haven, Conn., ca. 1880

the Governing Board was concerned in
that year.[31] The year 1925, the date of the
initial gift, marked the year in which Henry
and Raynham Townshend came jointly into
possession of the family's goods following
the death of their aunt Mary Buckelew
Townshend, after which they would have
been entitled to make a gift of the work. It
had, nonetheless, been at Yale for decades
before that moment. A recently discovered
photograph (fig. 10), showing the painting
already in situ at the Yale School of the
Fine Arts in the later nineteenth century,

indicates that the work had been placed
on deposit at Yale well before the date
of the formal gift. In the nineteenth and
early twentieth centuries, Yale's painting collections were considered part of
the School of the Fine Arts, but with
the opening of its own building in 1928,
the Gallery of Fine Arts (now the Yale
University Art Gallery) began to have a
degree of independence. The Townshend
painting, like all those from the School of
the Fine Arts, was eventually transferred
to the Gallery.

The Townshends are an old New Haven family. Both brothers, and many other members of the family, had earned degrees at Yale, and Raynham, a doctor, offered a class in anatomy to the students at the School of the Fine Arts. There is, unfortunately, no record of how the painting had come into the possession of the family, but here, too, we can offer some speculation. Henry and Raynham were the sons of Captain Charles Hervey Townshend, one of the great American merchant sailors of the nineteenth century, who sailed repeatedly from New Haven to Europe. The old lining canvas and the stretcher of the painting are thought to be English, of the mid-nineteenth century, while the frame in which the work came to Yale, made to fit the painting at its current, cut-down dimensions, is American and of the mid- or late nineteenth century.[32] The most reasonable assumption is that the painting came from Europe aboard one of Charles Townshend's ships, was framed in America, was eventually placed on deposit at Yale, and was later given to the University.[33] Efforts to find other references to the painting in America or in England during the nineteenth century have not yet been successful.[34]

Despite having been at Yale perhaps as early as the late 1870s, the *Education of the Virgin* was virtually unknown until its initial publication in 2010. Because of its condition it was rarely if ever exhibited after the Gallery moved from its Street Hall building to its new quarters in 1928, but the painting has not been entirely without attention since that time. In 1963 the canvas was sent to the restorer Morton Bradley, who removed much of the old repaint (he uncovered the partial angel at the top of the canvas, which was still painted out when the 1946 photograph was taken); in the context of the Charles Seymour–led conservation campaign then underway at Yale, Bradley was probably instructed only to strip off all overpainting and to do nothing more.[35] In 1970–71 Humberto Rodriguez-Camilloni, then a graduate student in the Department of the History of Art at Yale, studied the painting and noted its similarity to the early works by Velázquez. He sent photographs printed from the murky 1946 negative to one or two scholars, but received rather curt responses and appears to have pursued his ideas no further.

Despite its long neglect, the Yale *Education of the Virgin* is now, with the present exhibition, brought for the first time to a broad public. Presented here not only in its art-historical context but also with the technical information of its recent conservation treatment made available, the painting is of vital importance for our understanding of early Sevillian Baroque painting and specifically for our understanding of Velázquez's development. While it would be impossible to add to the reputation of Velázquez, considered by many to be among the greatest painters of the European tradition, the further study of the *Education of the Virgin*, created at the dawn of the artist's career, can perhaps lead us to a still greater appreciation of his genius.

This article covers much of the same ground as that in which the present author originally published the Yale canvas; see Marciari 2010. Some repetition of that article is unavoidable, but there are also some details and arguments covered there that are not repeated here, and so the curious reader is referred to that publication as well.

1. Pacheco 1990, 582–83. Roelas's picture has been variously dated to some time in the early 1610s (e.g., Valdivieso González 1978, 89, as ca. 1610–15; Valdivieso González, in Seville and Bilbao 2005–6, 78, as ca. 1615–16; and Seville 2008–9, cat. 24, as ca. 1610–15), but Pacheco's commentary would seem to corroborate a date contemporary with the completion of the convent's renovation in 1612.

2. On the cult of Saint Anne and the iconography of the Education of the Virgin, see Sheingorn 1993; Bergmann 2008; and Black 2010.

3. This typical aspect of Velázquez's early paintings is also highlighted by Keith 2006, 72, and by Pericolo 2011, 524–25.

4. Although often dated to the mid-1620s, after Velázquez's move to Madrid, the *Supper at Emmaus* is surely a picture of the Sevillian period, as proven by Hale 2005.

5. An often-cited passage in Pacheco's *Arte de la pintura* describes Velázquez's use of live models; see Pacheco 1990, 527–28. It might be noted that the heads of the figures are not copied from one painting to the next, but rather that the same man—with high forehead, wrinkled brow, hooked nose, hollow cheeks, and full beard—seems to have modeled for a number of paintings; in the Yale canvas, he is given gray-white hair, presumably in accordance with the iconographic requirement that Joachim be an elderly man. Harris 1982, 46–51, also emphasizes the use of models and common props, noting that the head of the *Old Woman Cooking Eggs* is the same model who served for the *Kitchen Scene with Christ in the House of Martha and Mary*.

6. Some confusion regarding this technique has been caused by the inaccurate description of the Yale painting by Jonathan Brown, in Brown 2010, who wrote that "[l]as arrugas de la frente de San Peterburgo tienen un sentido de relieve, mientras que en el de Yale parece como si fueran aplicadas mecánicamente encima de la piel" (the wrinkles of the forehead of the Saint Petersburg painting have a sense of relief, while those in the Yale painting seem as though they were mechanically applied over the skin; author's translation).

7. Pacheco 1990, 582–83.

8. As is sometimes noted—for example by the later iconographer Juan Interián de Ayala (see Black 2010, 188)—there is an inherent problem in the Education of the Virgin iconography, for apocryphal tradition held that the Virgin was sent to the temple at the age of three and was therefore no longer in her parents' home when she would have been old enough to be taught how to read. Given that there was, however, a desire among patrons for images of the Education, a younger girl would have at least seemed more appropriate to the scene.

9. Pericolo 2011, 524.

10. Much of the discussion of the painting to date has been carried out in the popular press rather than in scholarly journals: see Brown 2010; Díaz Padrón 2010; and Navarrete Prieto 2010. Tiffany 2012, 9–11, echoes Brown's rejection of the Yale picture and also rejects other newly proposed attributions to Velázquez such as the *Saint John the Baptist* at the Art Institute of Chicago and the *Immaculate Conception* at the Centro Velázquez in Seville; for a brief summary of the recent expansion of Velázquez's canon, see Marciari 2013a.

11. See Pericolo 2011, esp. pp. 524–25.

12. For more on this, see the essay "*The Education of the Virgin*: A Conservation Narrative and Technical Examination" in this catalogue.

13. The Budapest painting has long been attributed to Velázquez but has been, in the opinion of the present author, rightly questioned in recent years, for example, by Cherry 2006, 856, and London 2006–7, 118. The three or four other derivative versions of the painting are likewise typically lifeless (for these pictures, see Edinburgh 1996, cats. 26–29). On the problem of Velázquez's Sevillian workshop, see Harris 1996.

14. See Brown 2010.

15. Serrera 1996, 38. A version of the subject by Juan de Roelas, also painted in 1619, is even more closely related to Fernández's painting; one wonders whether it might not have been an intermediate model.

16. London 2006–7, cat. 10. The Hermitage *Tavern Scene* has also been linked to earlier engraved sources.

17. For the altarpiece, formerly in the church of San
Juan de la Palma, see Valdivieso González and
Serrera 1985, 193 and 223, no. 74.

18. On Pacheco's academy and the intellectual culture
in which the young Velázquez came of age, see
especially Tiffany 2012; regarding that study, see also
Marciari 2013a. For Velázquez's departure from the
painting traditions of Pacheco, see Bassegoda 1999
and Harris 2000.

19. The connections between Spanish Baroque naturalism in painting and sculpture were brilliantly
highlighted in London and Washington 2009–10;
see especially Xavier Bray's introductory essay,
pp. 15–43.

20. There is considerable bibliography on the importance
of Caravaggesque naturalism for the development
of Baroque painting in Seville. For examples, see
David Davies, in Edinburgh 1996; Benedetti 2005;
Seville and Bilbao 2005–6; Pericolo 2011, chap. 16;
and Rome 2011–12 (in a review of that exhibition, the
present author first advanced the idea of a formative
trip to Toledo, an argument further developed here;
see Marciari 2012). Brown 1986, 12–13, argues against
links between Caravaggio and Velázquez.

21. For Pacheco's travels, see Bassegoda 1999, 127; and
Fallay d'Este 2001, 227–30.

22. Madrid 2009, 110–41.

23. For more on the relationship between these two
works, see the essay "*The Education of the Virgin* and the
Shaping of Early Naturalism" in this catalogue.

24. There seem also to be parallels between the
Sevillian works of Velázquez and those of the
Italian painter Bartolomeo Cavarozzi, who traveled
to Spain in 1617–19. The latter's *Supper at Emmaus*
(J. Paul Getty Museum, Los Angeles), for example,
has been compared to the Hermitage *Tavern Scene*
(see Benedetti 2005, 66–69; despite the earlier attribution of the Getty painting to Giovanni Battista
Crescenzi, suggested by Marini 1981, the attribution
to Cavarozzi is now universally accepted). Moreover,
Cavarozzi's *Saint John the Baptist* in the cathedral at
Toledo can be linked to the *Saint John the Baptist* at
the Art Institute of Chicago, which has been convincingly reattributed to Velázquez (Zuccari, Véliz,
and Fiedler 2005; Cherry 2006, 856; Javier Portús
Pérez and Peter Cherry, in Madrid 2007, 245–46,
and cat. 9; and Portús Pérez 2009). The several
Spanish versions of Cavarozzi's *Mystical Marriage
of Saint Catherine*, one of which is in the convent of
Santa Paula, Seville, can also be brought into this
discussion. Yet, these paintings date to 1617–19, and
they may not have been formative influences on
Velázquez but rather coincidental works that document a broader trend in art in Spain. On Cavarozzi,
see Turin 2005–6.

25. Brown and Kagan 1987.

26. Seville and Bilbao 2005–6, cat. 24. If by Pablo Legot,
as suggested by Cherry 2006, 856, the work would
probably postdate Velázquez's Sevillian paintings.

27. For these debates, see Pericolo 2011, chap. 16.

28. Passolas Jáuregui 1997, 51–52; and Morales 2004,
1:238–39.

29. The London *Immaculate Conception* and *Saint John*
were first recorded in 1800 at the convent of Shod
Carmelites (Ceán Bermúdez 1800, 5:179) and must
have been a Carmelite commission, as is argued
persuasively by Tiffany 2012, chap. 1.

30. Glendinning 1989, 118.

31. The "style of Murillo" label given to the works in
the donation document is a generic label for a painting of the Sevillian school. The gift was of two pictures. There is no otherwise-unprovenanced second
picture still in the collection that corresponds to
the description, but a deaccessioned "Holy Family,
Spanish, seventeenth century" sold at the Plaza Art
Gallery, New York, February 22, 1946, lot 321, must
have been the other. Again, the coincidence of a
1946 date seems to tie the records together.

32. The painting was placed in a more stylistically
appropriate frame following the recent conservation
treatment.

33. The Townshends of New Haven are indirect
descendants of the Marquesses Townshend of
Raynham Hall in Norfolk, which once had a notable
collection of paintings, but no pictures came
from Norfolk to New Haven prior to 1926, when
Henry Hotchkiss Townshend purchased Sir Joshua
Reynolds's portrait of the first Marquess Townshend
from his then-impoverished cousins. The New
Haven Townshends are not thought to be relations
of the Joseph Townsend who in 1791 published *A
Journey through Spain*.

34. Although Americans had begun to collect Spanish
painting in the nineteenth century, there was very

little taste for Baroque religious painting of this type, so the acquisition remains mysterious. See Reist and Colomer 2012; and Marciari 2013b.

35. On the history of conservation at Yale, see Garland 2003.

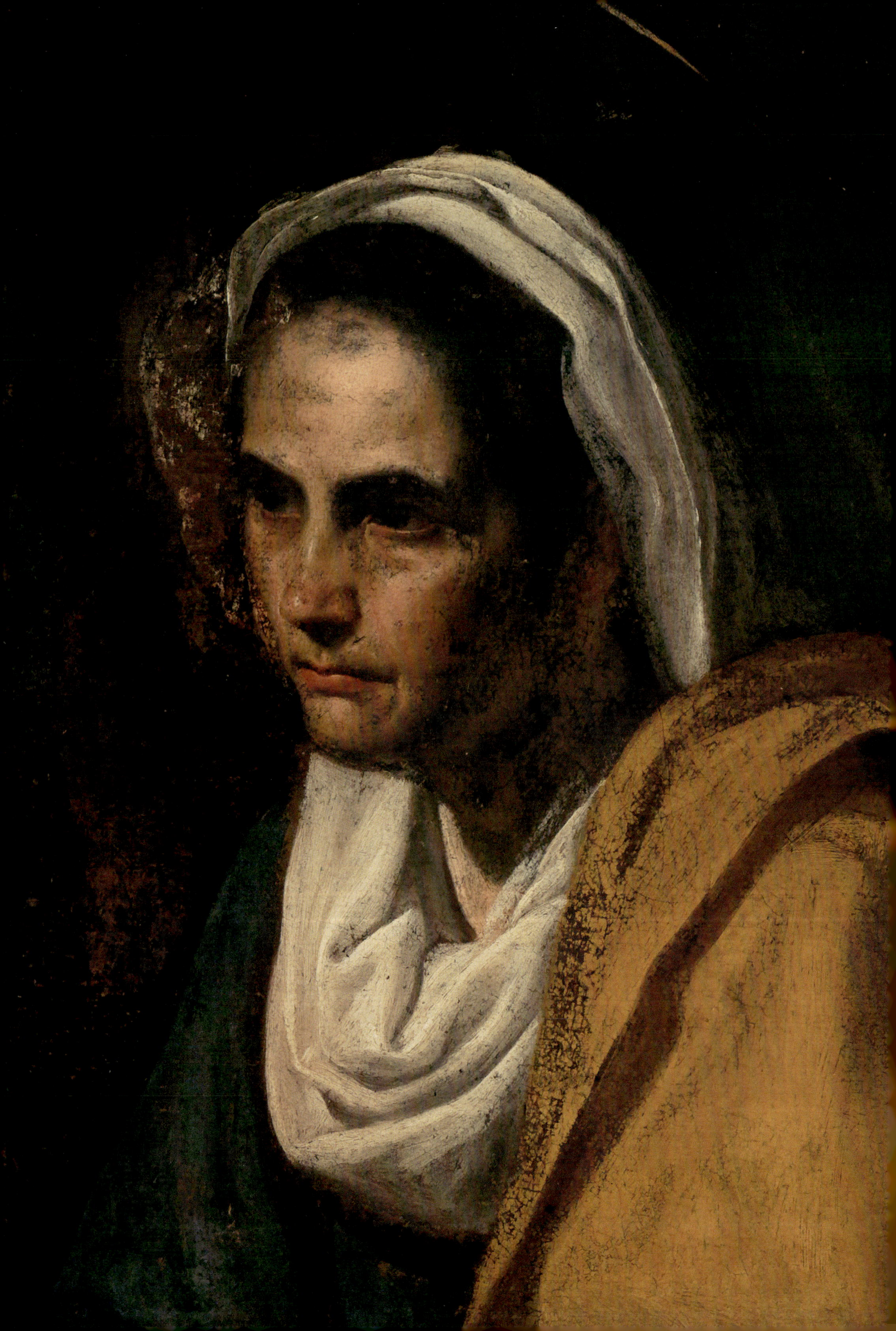

THE EDUCATION OF THE VIRGIN

A Conservation Narrative and Technical Examination

CARMEN ALBENDEA, IAN MCCLURE,
ANIKÓ BEZUR, and JENS STENGER

In the summer of 2012, the conservation and technical examination of the *Education of the Virgin*, a painting attributed to Diego Velázquez by John Marciari in his article of 2010, began in earnest. The technical examination, undertaken by the Yale University Art Gallery's Conservation Department and the research laboratory of Yale's Institute for the Preservation of Cultural Heritage, revealed a considerable amount of information about the technique and materials of the painting and supported Marciari's attribution to Velázquez.

The first record of the painting is contained in a photograph from around 1880 (see Marciari, fig. 10). The photograph shows the painting already reduced in size, with the remaining half of the angel at the top painted out. The marks of the horizontal crossbar of the original strainer—visible in the image of the painting before restoration (fig. 1)—which would have been placed across the center, now lie about 12 cm above the center of the painting. Assuming that about 3 cm is required to complete the cat and dog at the bottom of the work, about 28 cm would need to be added to the top of the painting to place the horizontal crossbar across its center. As the painting is currently 168 × 137 cm, this would suggest that the original dimensions of the painting were approximately 200 × 140 cm.[1] The X-radiograph of the painting (fig. 2) clearly shows cusping of the fabric on each vertical side, indicating that the painting is close to its original width.[2] Although much less accentuated compared to the sides, cusping is also visible at the lower edge of the canvas, which confirms the impression that only a small amount of the support has been removed and that the cat and the dog were always positioned close to the bottom of the canvas.

The painting has sustained a history of damage and neglect. The original fabric has a long vertical tear near the upper-left corner, and numerous smaller tears and scores appear

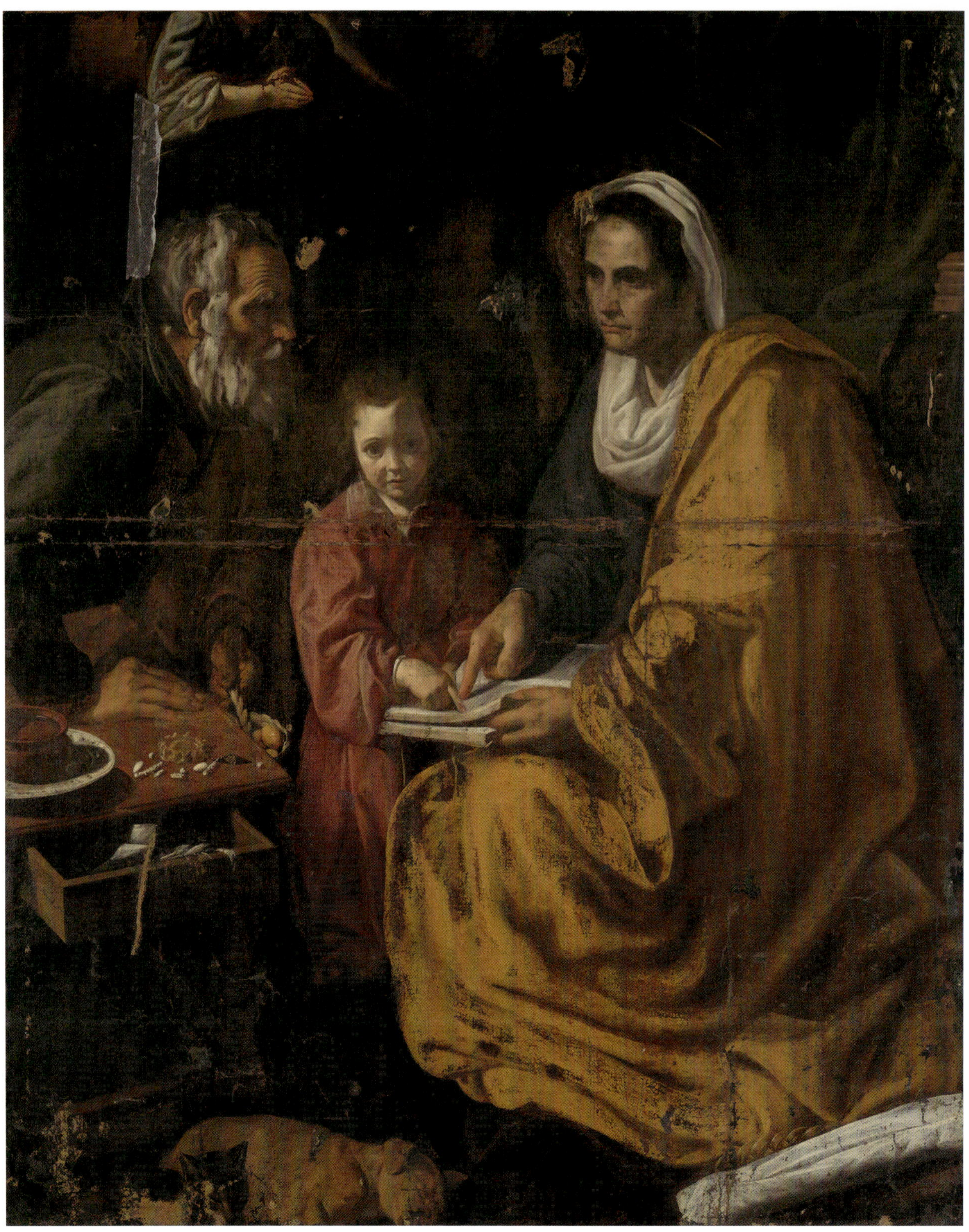

Fig. 1. Diego Velázquez, *The Education of the Virgin* (before restoration)

in the paint surface. A piece of plain-weave canvas has been inserted at top left, to replace a missing portion of the original, complex-weave fabric. The losses to the paint layer along the position of the original strainer's crossbar also suggest that the canvas had become very slack, even partly detached from its support, allowing it to sag over the crossbar. However, other than a photograph in the Gallery's curatorial files taken in 1946, no clear record of the condition and treatment of the painting survives before it was sent for cleaning in 1963 to Morton Bradley in Arlington, Massachusetts. At that time, the angel was discovered, as was the considerable damage to the paint layers, and Bradley returned the painting, cleaned but unrestored. The damage he revealed—areas where the upper layers of paint had been thinned and patches that had been completely removed—suggests that very alkaline materials were once used to clean the painting, possibly potash and lye, a common practice in the eighteenth and nineteenth centuries.[3] Bradley left numerous old fillings and areas of overpaint undisturbed.[4]

Upon its return to Yale, the painting received little attention, until 2004, when John Marciari, then the Gallery's Nina and Lee Griggs Associate Curator of Early European Art, attributed the painting—previously catalogued as "Spanish School" and misidentified as a Holy Family—to Velázquez. The painting was once more considered for restoration. In 2005 preliminary material analysis was undertaken, overpaint and an old natural resin varnish were partly removed, and restoration began.[5] However, in 2006 the treatment was put on hold to allow further technical examination and a wider discussion about its attribution and treatment options.

The publication in 2010 of Marciari's article in *Ars Magazine* stirred international interest in the painting.[6] With a history of supporting university projects worldwide, including initiatives at Yale, the Spanish banking group Banco Santander provided funding for a thorough examination of the condition and conservation of the painting, and a technical study of both its materials and technique compared to those found in other works from Velázquez's Sevillian period.[7] The expansion of the Gallery's Conservation Department beginning in 2008 and the establishment of the research laboratory of the Center for Conservation and Preservation, part of Yale's Institute for the Preservation of Cultural Heritage, also provided the opportunity for a more focused and sustained project. The bank funded the appointment of a conservator who would be fluent in technical conservation terms in both Spanish and English, which would make best use of this opportunity for comparative research.[8]

After a brief exhibition at the Gallery from December 2010 to February 2011, the restoration carried out between 2005 and 2006 was removed, as was the existing temporary varnish and a very discolored layer thought to be glue, applied to the surface of the painting to saturate it after the existing lining was completed. These

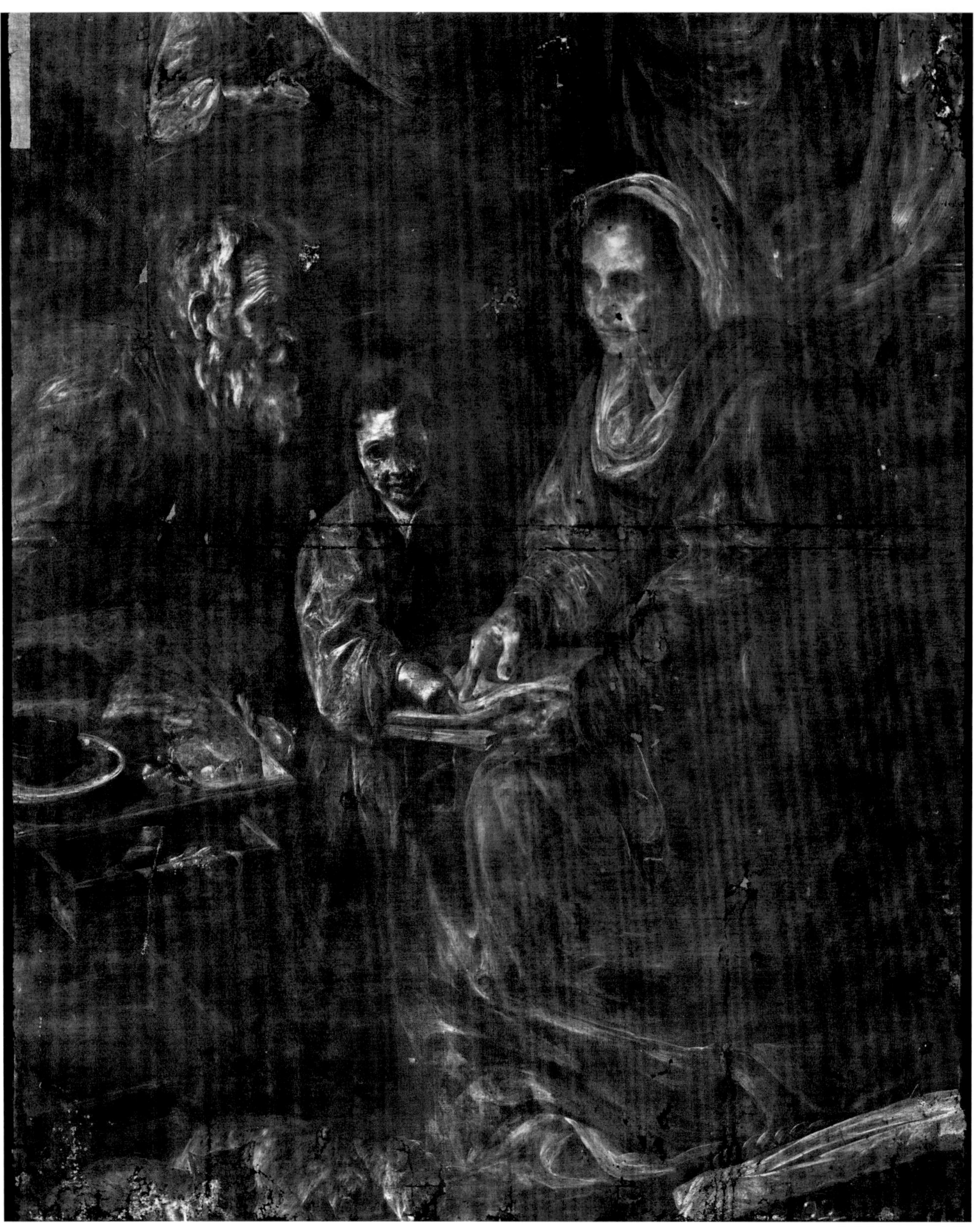

Fig. 2. X-radiograph of the *Education of the Virgin*

steps improved the legibility of the painting. The decision was then made to remove the existing lining, slightly modifying and reusing the mid-nineteenth-century stretcher that was now supporting the painting, the original strainer having been discarded during some previous treatment. Simon Bobak, an internationally recognized expert in traditional lining methods, came from England to inspect the painting and, over the course of three visits in 2012, removed the lining and relined the painting onto a new linen support, with a glue-paste adhesive. This greatly reduced the cupped paint surface and brought the raised tears in the canvas into alignment. The X-radiograph shown in figure 2 was then made before the canvas was returned to its stretcher so that the stretcher would not be included in the X-radiograph and disrupt the image.[9] With the paint surface condition more stable, conservators at the Gallery removed further overpaint, revealing small but significant details such as the muzzle of the cat. Some areas of overpaint were left as found, since it was deemed impossible to remove them without damaging the original paint. The abraded paint of the shadow under the fold of Saint Anne's cloak as it passes over her proper-left shoulder, for example, had been overpainted in a much earlier restoration attempt with now-insoluble ochre paint; this distortion was corrected by glazing during the present restoration. Paint losses were then filled with a gypsum-gelatin putty and textured to match the original surface. The painting has been restored to a level that achieves a consistent legibility of the image, without attempting to remove all traces of wear and damage (see pl. 1).

The areas of abrasion and loss in the painting have offered a unique opportunity to study aspects of its creation that would otherwise have remained invisible. However, the interpretation of the painting in its present state has to be approached with caution, as much of what is now visible was never intended by the artist to be seen and much that was intended to be seen has either been abraded or removed through damage and previous misguided cleaning.

The X-radiograph provides a very detailed image of the painting.[10] This is due to the low X-ray density of the ground, which is composed largely of earth-based pigments that are transparent to X-rays. This makes the lead white–containing paint layers, which absorb X-rays, very distinct, and other pigments, less dense than lead white, visible. In the X-radiograph, certain passages of the painting appear more vigorously worked compared to what is visible on the surface in normal light, which seems much flatter and more subdued. This loss of definition is due to the abrasion of glazes and thin paint layers on the surface (in the ochre mantle, for example); to the darkening of glazes on the paint surface, which obscures the paint layers underneath (on the green curtain);[11] and to obvious changes in the composition (in the lower part of the ochre mantle).

The painting is painted on a *mantelillo veneciano*, a patterned fabric that was used as a support for oil paintings by Spanish

artists during the sixteenth century, and
which became more widespread in the first
half of the seventeenth century (fig. 3).[12]
Mantelillos were woven in broad widths,
which made them ideal for large paintings
because they could be used whole, without
the visually obtrusive seams created by
joining narrower canvases. They were
considered more appropriate for significant
commissions, particularly religious works.
Velázquez used this type of fabric support
for some commissions, mainly religious,

and does not seem to have used it after he
finally left Seville in 1624.[13] A contract, for
example, signed by Francisco Pacheco and
Velázquez in 1623 for an altarpiece specifies
the use of *mantel* for the center image of
the Immaculate Conception.[14]

The *mantelillo* of the *Education of
the Virgin* was sized with a glue preparation to seal the fibers. This medium-rich,
nonparticulate brown sizing layer is visible
in a cross-section sample that includes
the support (fig. 4). As can also be seen

Fig. 3. Detail of the reverse of the *Education of the Virgin,* showing the diamond
pattern of the *mantelillo veneciano* and the dark stain in the canvas, which might be
connected to water damage that occurred sometime before the painting was lined

in this image, a dull brown ground com-
prising a heterogeneous mixture of silica,
calcium carbonate, and dolomite, as well as
magnesium-containing alumino-silicates,
iron oxides, and lead white, was applied in
two or three layers to the canvas.[15] Both
the appearance and the composition of the
ground in the Yale painting are consistent
with *tierra* or *barro de Sevilla*, a local clay that
Pacheco praises and recommends in his *Arte
de la pintura* and that many Sevillian artists,
including Velázquez, used to prepare their
canvases. Indentations of different lengths
and shapes—never intended to be seen
but now apparent to the naked eye due to
abrasion and thinning of the paint layers—
are found on the ground layer throughout
the painting, suggesting that it may have
been applied with a knife, a technique
recommended by Pacheco as well.[16] Similar
marks have been found in the grounds of
Velázquez's Sevillian paintings.

On top of the ground layer, a thin,
slightly translucent, reddish-brown layer was
evenly applied. This layer was detected when
examining the painting under the stereomicroscope, and its presence was confirmed in
cross sections. This double preparation might
seem unusual for Velázquez in a painting
from his Sevillian period; however, double
preparations have been detected in other
paintings from the artist's early period, which
suggests that Velázquez was not as strict
or methodical with his grounds as is often
thought.[17] The purpose of this *imprimatura*
layer was probably to darken the dull brown
ground color to obtain deeper shadows,
thereby creating a more dramatic contrast

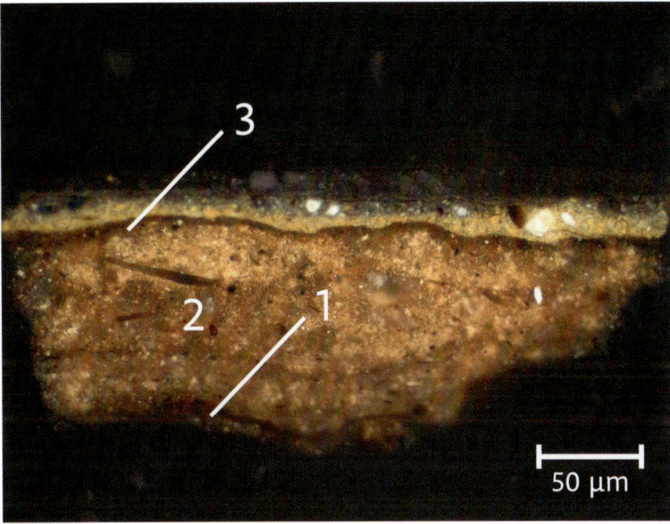

of light and dark. Microscopy and elemental
analysis indicate that this layer contains fairly
coarse azurite and calcium carbonate grains
in a matrix of fine red and brown iron oxides,
silica, and alumino-silicate (clay) particles.[18]
Close visual examination of exposed areas of
the *imprimatura* and of polished cross sections
indicates that a black pigment is also present.
The admixture suggests the use of palette
scrapings.[19]

Although the dark ground and *imprimatura* certainly play an important role in
the final appearance of the painting, adding
depth to the shadows and intensifying the
opacity of the lighter colors, the artist does
not seem to have made use of the *imprimatura* in the actual painting stage by leaving
it exposed. Instead, he consistently applied
paint over it in areas of shadow, even if just
a thin wash.[20] The color of the *imprimatura*

Fig. 4. Cross section of the top edge of the
background of the *Education of the Virgin*, showing
1) the brown sizing layer on top of the canvas;
2) the dull brown ground applied in several layers;
and 3) the thin reddish-brown *imprimatura*

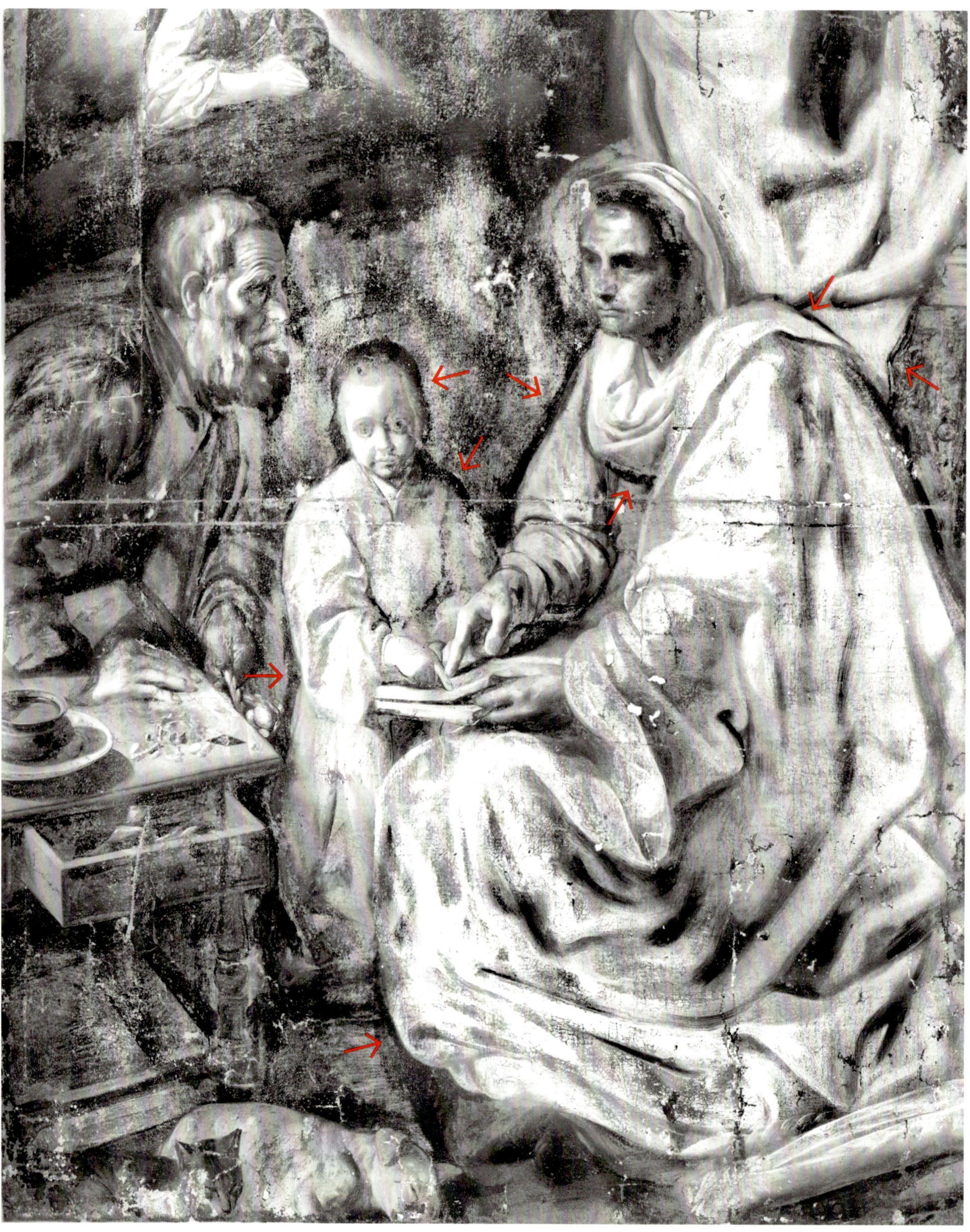

Fig. 5. Infrared reflectogram of the *Education of the Virgin*, at 1700 nm, showing
the broad, brushy dark lines of underdrawing

is visible today only in areas of abrasion or where the application of the paint around contours was not executed precisely. Where the ground is exposed—for example, around Saint Anne's head and in areas of the background—blanching is apparent; blanching often occurs in grounds composed of *barro de Sevilla* or Sevillian clay, most likely due to the presence of hygroscopic clay compounds, which cause the ground to be sensitive to moisture.[21]

The composition of the work was outlined in a variety of ways in preparation for painting. Most obvious and clearly visible to the naked eye and with infrared reflectography is the sketching of the design in some areas with broad dark brown to black fluidly brushed lines (fig. 5). These are generally painted over the *imprimatura* layer, and they are sometimes deliberately left uncovered in parts of the contours of figures and objects. These lines are not to be confused with the similarly fluid dark lines used in later stages to correct or reinforce contours, visible to the naked eye in the final painting.

Also visible with infrared, although much less apparent against the dark ground, are some thinner dark lines that may have been used for areas that required more precise and detailed underdrawing, such as hands or facial features. The clearest examples are visible in the hands of Saint Anne—for example, on the contour of her proper-right index finger (fig. 6)—or the line drawn between the Virgin's lips.

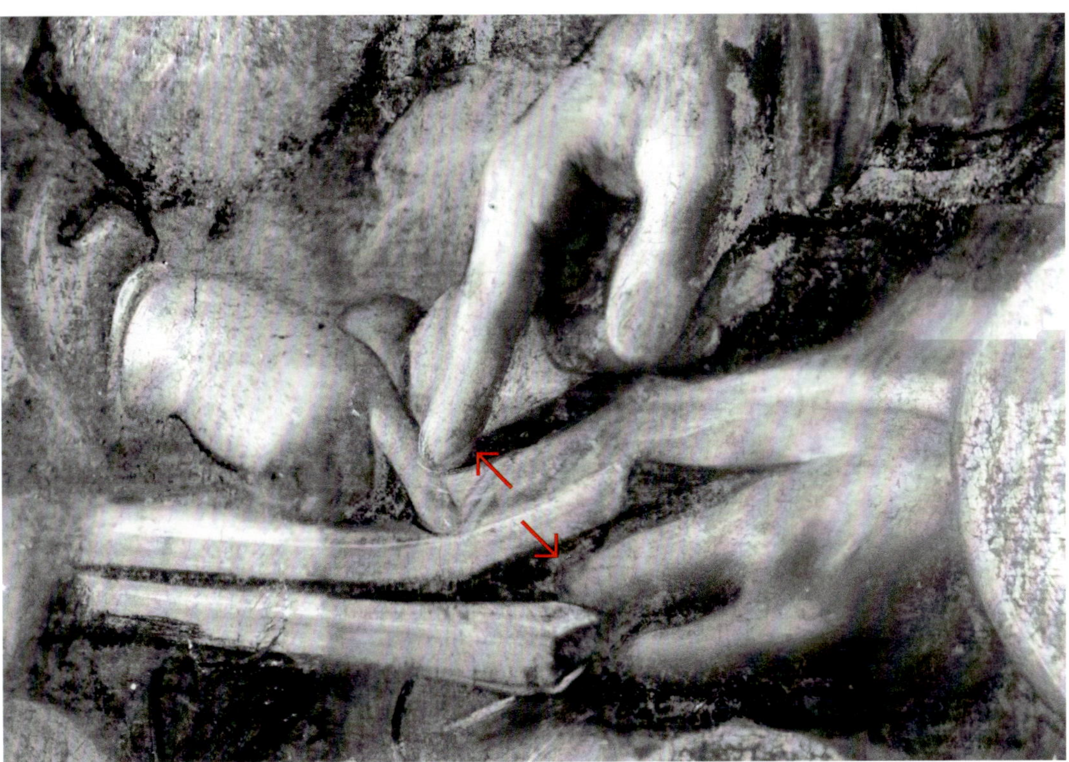

Fig. 6. Detail of the infrared reflectogram of the *Education of the Virgin,* showing the fine underdrawing lines in Saint Anne's hands

Some very thin, slightly raised, light-colored lines of varying lengths were also used to indicate the position of certain elements. These are likely the graphic lines that have been detected in seventeenth-century Spanish paintings, principally by Velázquez. Zahira Véliz was the first to identify these lines in Velázquez's early paintings, describing them as fine, raised, radio-opaque lines, probably drawn with a small, stiff brush used to draw the main contours of the composition at the underdrawing stage.[22] These lines are sometimes clearly visible with X-radiography (when painted with a radio-opaque pigment) but are imperceptible to the naked eye, as they are almost invariably covered by later paint. In general, only when the paint layer has been abraded, or in the rare instance where gaps in the paint leave them exposed, can they be seen.[23] In the Yale painting, some of these lines are white—for instance, the line delineating the front edge of the table, visible in the X-radiograph and through areas of abrasion when viewed under the microscope (fig. 7)—but other shorter, colored lines painted in iron-based pigments, transparent to X-rays, have been exposed in

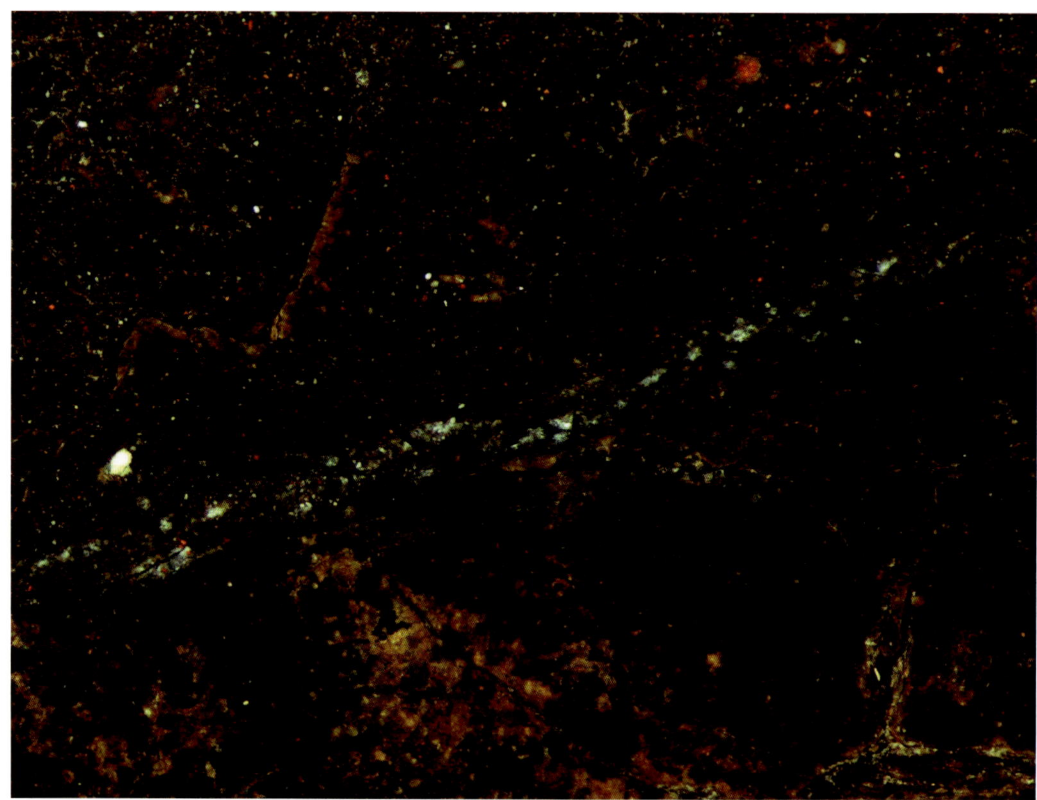

Fig. 7. Photomicrograph of the *Education of the Virgin*, showing the white graphic line (now visible due to the abrasion of the paint layers on top) used to position the front edge of the table

abraded areas—such as the line indicating the position of the Virgin's proper-left shoulder—and are now visible (fig. 8). Even with microscope examination, it is not clear whether these graphic lines were applied on top of the *imprimatura* or after the broad underdrawing had been sketched in.[24]

The artist also used a single, fine, thick-bodied, and generally radio-opaque line to delineate some contours during the subsequent painting process. These lines are easily confused with the preparatory graphic lines, since they have a very similar appearance, both in the X-radiograph and in raking light. However, careful observation under the microscope reveals that they were painted with the same color as the surrounding paint. Clear examples of these lines are found delineating Saint Joachim's forehead and the contours of the cat and dog. Other thin contour lines also appear in the X-radiograph, which, unlike single graphic lines, are ridges of paint produced along the edges of wider brushstrokes applied with a stiff brush. Examples of these lines are visible around the tip of Saint Anne's index finger and on the edges of the book (fig. 9).

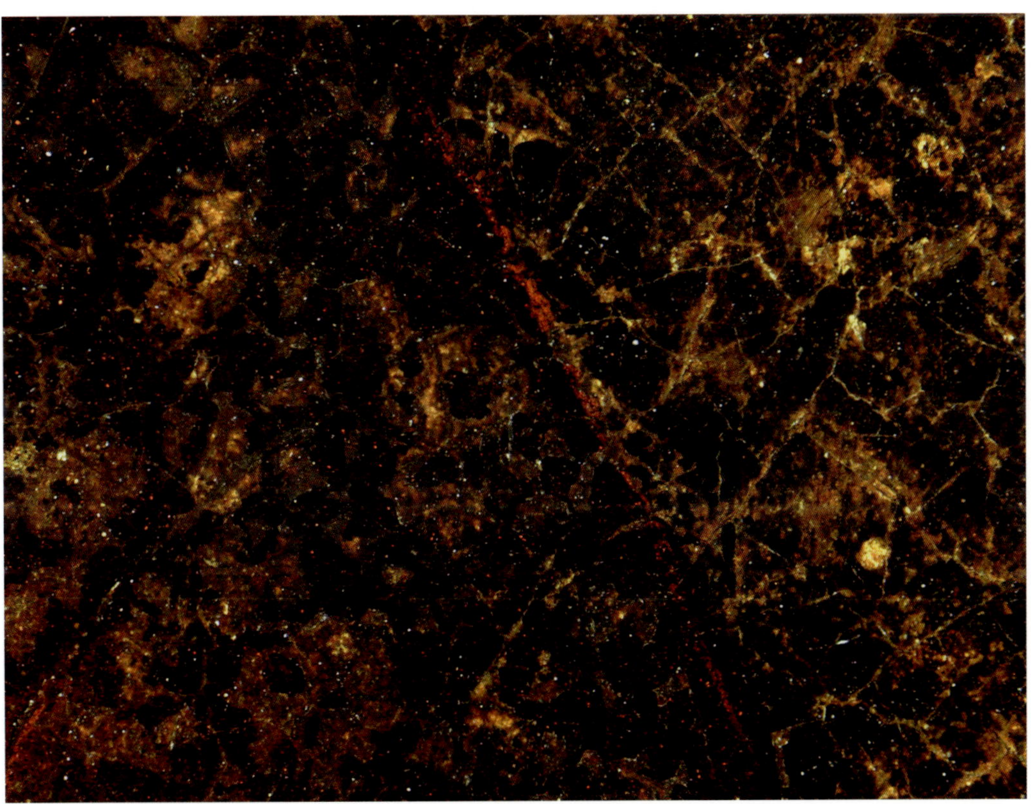

Fig. 8. Photomicrograph of the *Education of the Virgin*, showing the red graphic line used to position the Virgin's proper-left shoulder

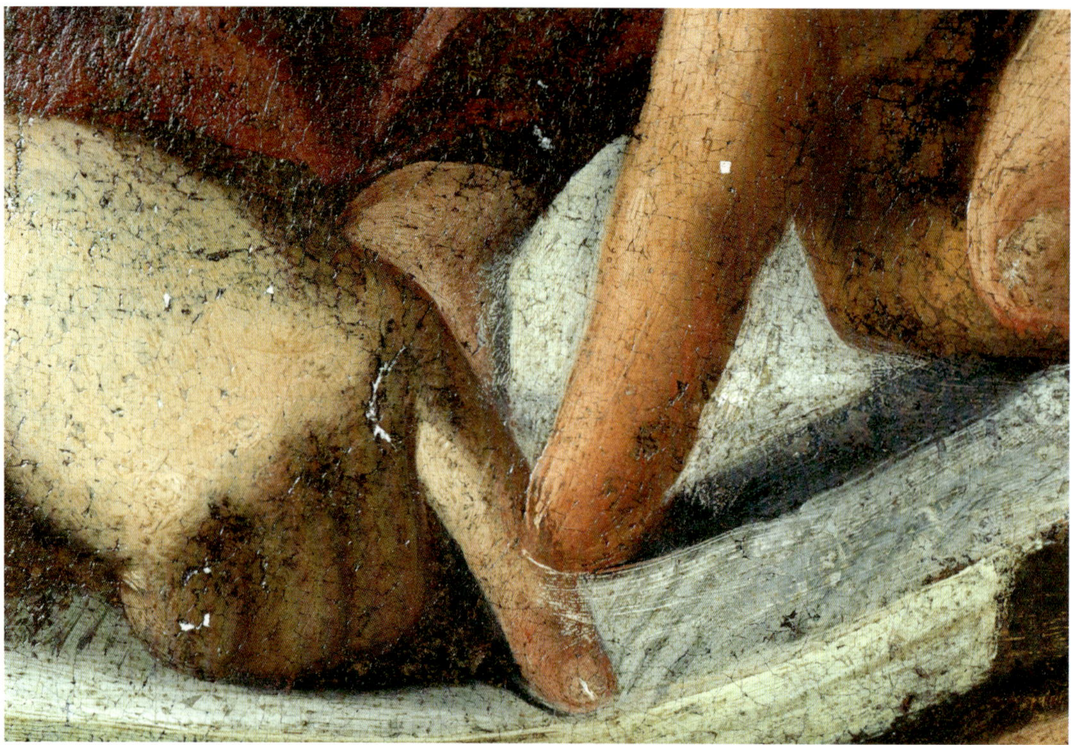

Fig. 9. Detail of the *Education of the Virgin* (before restoration), showing the ridges of paint, produced with a stiff brush, around the tip of Saint Anne's index finger

Dark lines were also used to correct and reinforce contours. These lines vary from broad and washlike, visible on the right edge of Saint Anne's ochre mantle and on her blue sleeve, refining the outlines, to thin and very dense, such as those used to define the lower edge of Saint Anne's mantle or the left outline of the Virgin's robe. The use of these lines reflects the artist's concern for distinguishing elements of the composition, a feature that he clearly shares with Pacheco and most Sevillian artists of the period.

The binding medium of the paint has been confirmed to be linseed oil, based on the ratios of palmitic and stearic acids.[25]

Analysis of the Yale painting indicates that the artist used a relatively simple pigment palette, clearly dominated by iron earth colors.[26] Red, orange, and brown earths, including umber,[27] red lake, azurite, smalt, yellow ochre, black (both carbon and bone black[28]), and lead white,[29] are the principal pigments that have been detected. This palette is consistent with Velázquez's Sevillian paintings.

The dominant color in the painting is the sweep of Saint Anne's mantle, painted in yellow ochre with umber to create shadows, similar to Velázquez's treatment of the robe in his *Saint Thomas* at the Musée des Beaux-Arts d'Orléans (see Marciari, fig. 7).[30] The robe of the Virgin is painted with lead white and red lake.[31] The use of an expensive pigment such as red lake in the painting is indicative of an important commission. During his Sevillian period, Velázquez seems to have used this pigment mainly for religious paintings. It is difficult to know to what extent the color of the red robe has altered, but compared to other organic red garments from Velázquez's early period (such as those of the *Immaculate Conception* [see Marciari, fig. 8] and *Saint John the Evangelist*, in the National Gallery, London, or the robe of the Virgin in the *Adoration of the Magi*, in the Museo Nacional del Prado, Madrid, among others), it appears to have faded substantially less. The degree of fading of the red in the Yale painting seems comparable to that of the *Immaculate Conception* from the Fundación Focus-Abengoa, Seville (see Navarette Prieto, fig. 6).

The artist used azurite for the sleeve of Saint Anne's blue dress.[32] When the artist changed the outline of the ochre robe so that the blue dress would be visible folded over her foot, the alteration was made in smalt, another blue pigment, also used for the decoration of the white plate. The areas painted with this pigment are now a dull gray-brown in appearance, typical of deteriorated smalt.[33] Tin and lead were detected in the yellow highlight of the jewel-like object on the edge of the drawer, suggesting the use of lead-tin yellow.[34] Microscopic examination revealed remnants of an orange-brown translucent material over certain paint passages, mainly over the ochre mantle. These could be residues of an original varnish or a glaze. Further analysis of this material is forthcoming.

Overall, the composition seems to have been developed from individual elements rather than having been conceived as a coherent, unified space, which accounts for some obvious inconsistences in terms of perspective, light, and scale. This bears comparison with the handling of perspective in the *Tavern Scene* at the State Hermitage Museum, Saint Petersburg (see Marciari, fig. 1), where the relation of the seated figures to the table is difficult to interpret spatially, as noted by John Marciari in his essay in this catalogue.

The handling of the paint in the Yale canvas varies from broader and thicker brushstrokes used for the draperies to looser and more vibrant touches perceptible in the smaller objects (the decoration and nails on the chair, and the objects on the table), and from the wet-in-wet and thicker application of the paint (the wrinkles on Saint Joachim's forehead) to the delicate feathery brushstrokes visible in some passages (the shadows in Saint Anne's hands).

The artist used a fairly direct painting technique with a simple layer structure in most of the passages, as in the Virgin's robe, painted directly over the *imprimatura*, modeling wet-in-wet paint from light to dark. Lighter and medium pink tones were painted first; the dark *imprimatura* was left in reserve for the darkest shadows, which were painted later. Some lighter shadows were created by glazing translucent red

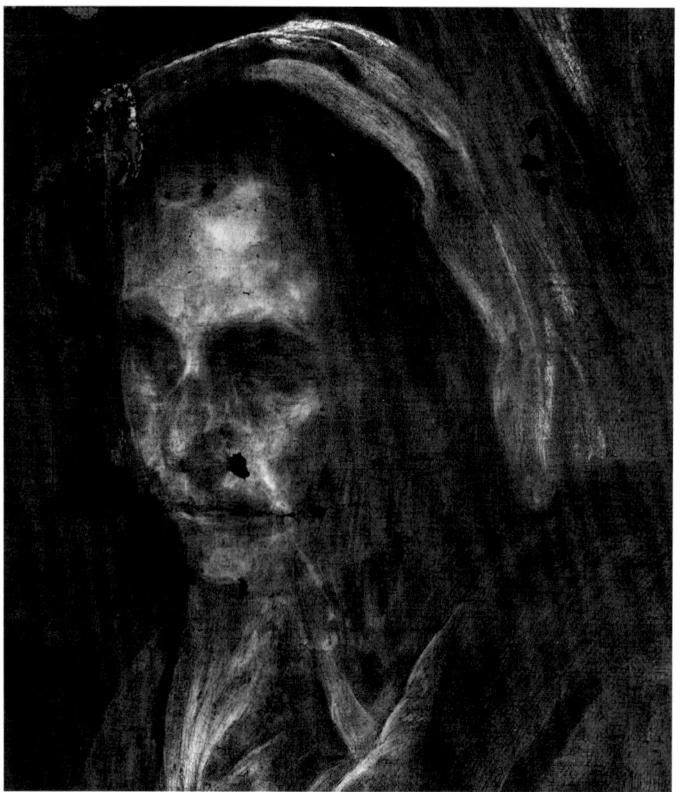

over opaque underlayers. Lastly, impastoed white highlights were applied, as well as rich brushstrokes of red lake to reinforce contours and deep shadows. Remnants of a very thin orange layer are visible under the microscope in shadowed areas, giving the fabric an iridescent effect, as in shot silk; a similar effect is

Fig. 10. Detail of the X-radiograph of the *Education of the Virgin*, showing a series of vertical and horizontal indentations/scratches on Saint Anne's proper-left cheek and jaw, probably a result of the artist scraping off paint layers before painting over them. Also visible are some illegible radio-opaque shapes in Saint Anne's chin and neck, most likely remnants of underpainting that had also been partially scraped off by the artist, and at top left, the original contour of the saint's head, which once was clearly more tilted toward the Virgin.

seen in the pink drapery of Saint Anne in Juan de Roelas's *Education of the Virgin* (pl. 2). Despite this direct painting technique, the final result is very complex, as many changes in the composition were made, suggesting that the artist had difficulty in combining all the elements of the composition satisfactorily. The only areas that do not seem to have undergone any major alterations during the painting stage are the table, green curtain, and chair. These elements were carefully painted directly over the reddish-brown *imprimatura* within the contours that were originally planned.

Pentimenti are now visible in the X-radiograph, with infrared reflectography, and to the naked eye. The artist chose to alter the composition by either painting directly over the first design or by scraping features off in some areas before applying a new paint layer. In at least one instance, he painted out the original design completely before laying-in the new and final paint layers. Nowhere is this more evident than in the development of Saint Anne's head. The artist first painted the head tilted more toward the Virgin. He then scraped away the paint in the areas of the fleash and headscarf and painted a new face, in a more upright position (fig. 10). This second attempt must also have proved unsatisfactory as it was painted out with black paint extending to her neck and ear, before the third and final version of the face was painted, with a slight adjustment to its contour. The raised outline of the second face is visible through the abrasion of the black paint at the edge of Saint Anne's face in the final painting (fig.

11). A somewhat similar technique was used in Velázquez's portrait of Philip IV in the Museo Nacional del Prado, Madrid, where the artist painted out the pentiment before applying the new layer of paint, but, instead of black paint, he used a reddish paint similar to that of the *imprimatura*.[35]

Other changes were made during the execution of the composition. Saint Anne's blue robe was originally intended to be seen over her proper-right leg. Remnants of blue paint were found under the book and, further down, under the ochre paint; it appears that the artist first painted this area with red lake, then scraped most of it off and painted over it with the dark blue. The saint's ochre mantle was significantly reduced at the bottom, leading to some now-indecipherable changes in the folds of the lower section and to the repainting of a section noted above, in smalt, which has now discolored substantially (fig. 12). The presence of dark red paint under parts of Saint Anne's blue robe and scarf (which appears to be the same as that used for the Virgin's robe) and traces of flesh-colored paint under her sleeve (likely remnants of a larger painted area that was scraped

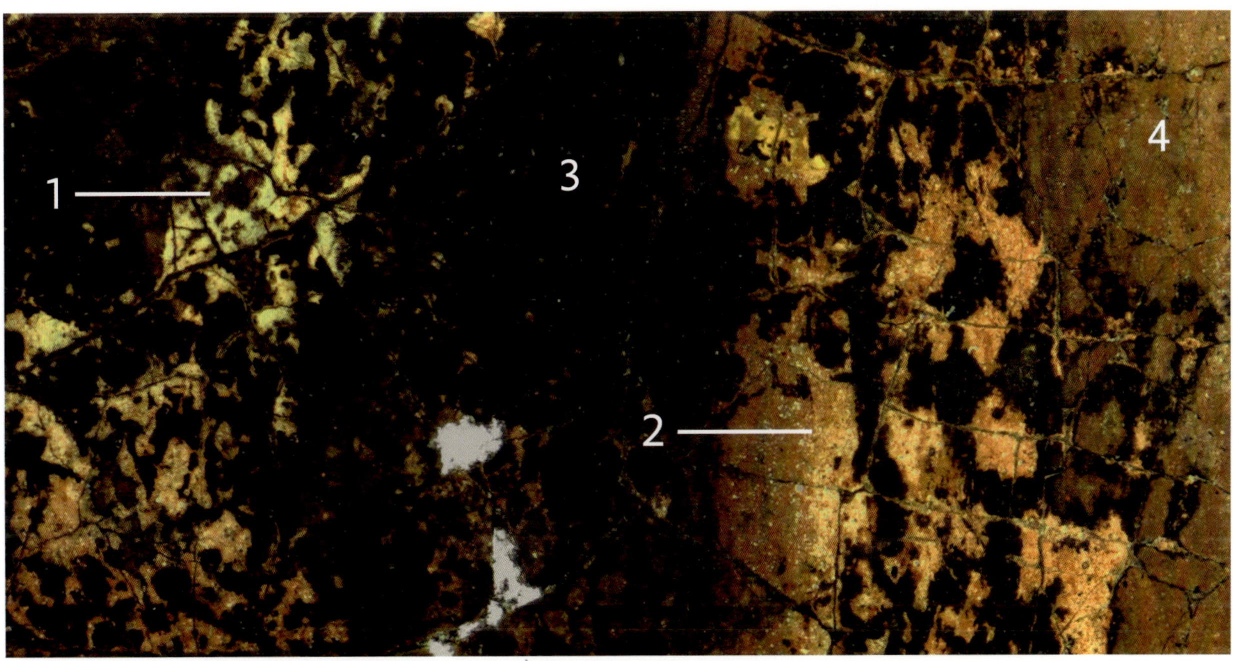

Fig. 11. Photomicrograph of the *Education of the Virgin* (before restoration), showing the three stages in the depiction of Saint Anne's head, including 1) the painting of the first version of Saint Anne's face, which was mostly scraped off; 2) the painting of the second version of the face; 3) the black layer covering the second version of the face and remnants of the first version; and 4) the final version

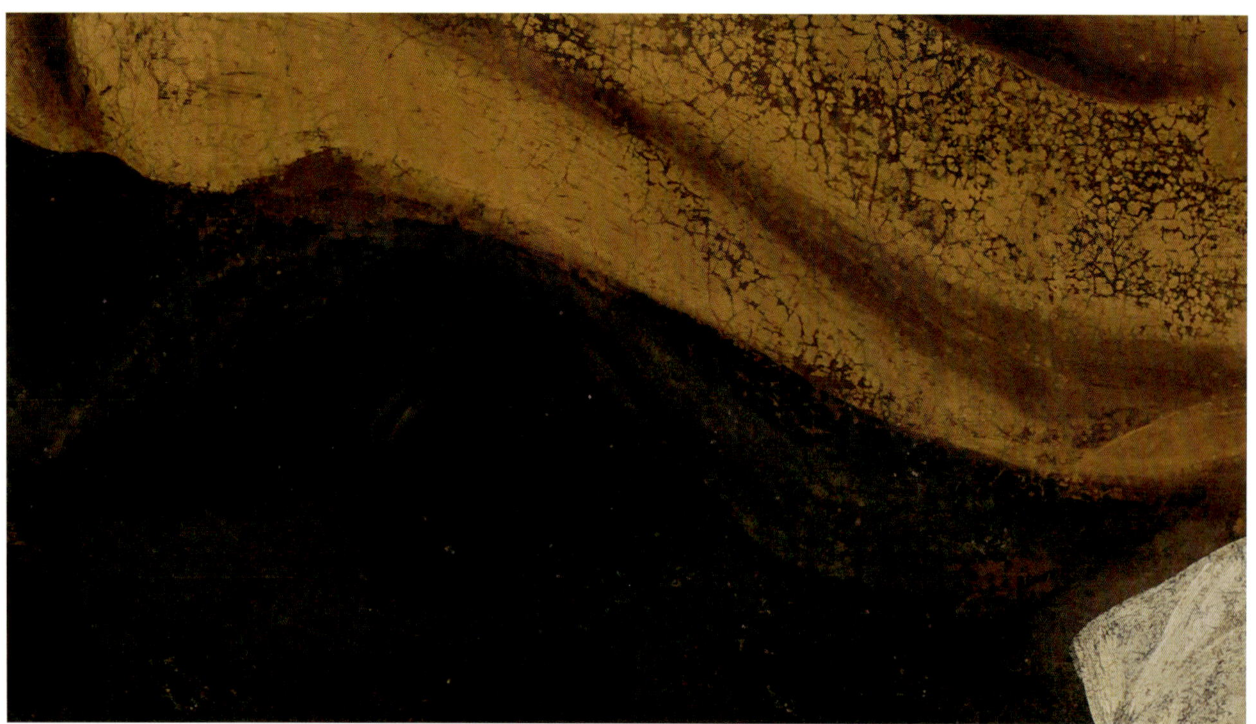

Fig. 12. Detail of the *Education of the Virgin*, showing the degradation of the blue pigment smalt on the lower part of Saint Anne's robe

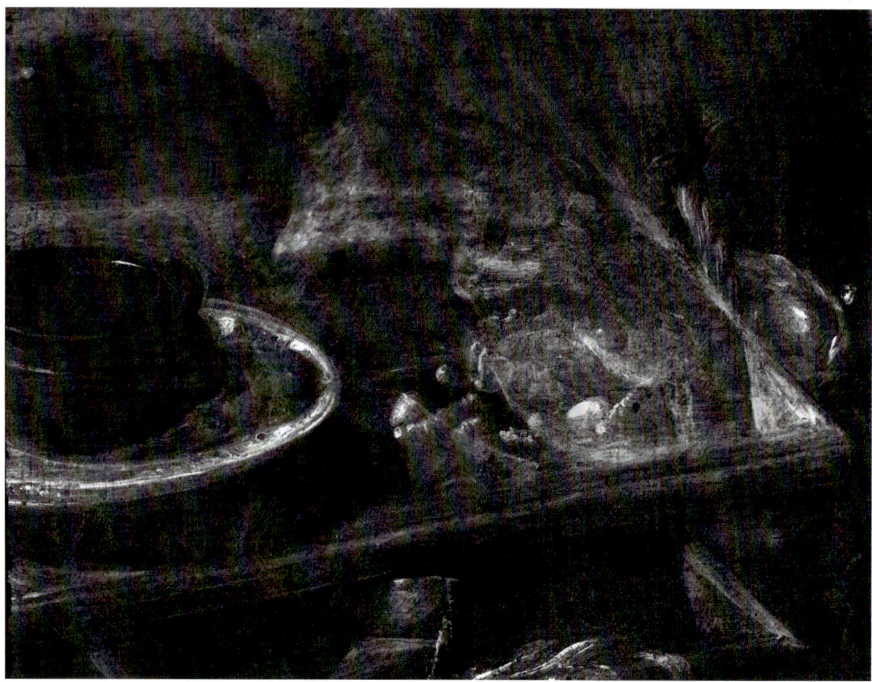

Fig. 13. Detail of the X-radiograph of the *Education of the Virgin*, showing the changes in the composition to the objects on the front-right corner of the table

off) might suggest a different posture for the Virgin, leaning toward her mother, or even trial "brush wipings," as the Virgin was painted before the figure of Saint Anne.[36] More complex changes that are difficult to interpret with any of the imaging techniques employed were made to the area around the tabletop. The X-radiograph shows that Saint Joachim's proper-right arm was not originally conceived in its current position: it was not initially intended to be seen over the table. There is evidence of a round shape under Saint Joachim's arm, suggesting that a bowl or jug of some sort was originally planned in this space. Direct examination of the area under the microscope reveals that the pentiment has a very painterly and textured appearance; the brushwork is very bold and impastoed. There are a number of colors lying next to each other (cream, orange, red, gray, khaki green, pink). Furthermore, there is a radio-opaque shape with round contours at the front-right corner of the table, now painted out (fig. 13). Some experts see in this shape a loaf of bread similar to that painted by Velázquez in some of his *bodegones*—for example, in the Hermitage *Tavern Scene*. However, the range of colors of the pentiment, visible through the abrasion of the paint layers, makes this unlikely. To the left of this shape, there is another radio-opaque form that might be interpreted as a cloth. Both of these shapes on the front-right corner of the table were replaced in the final painting stage with a series

of objects similar to those in Roelas's *Education*. The only two objects that the artist originally intended to place on the table are the earthenware bowl and the plate, as they were both painted directly on top of the *imprimatura*. As a result of the numerous changes that took place in this area, there are many inconsistencies in terms of perspective and lighting, the most obvious ones being the awkward positioning of Saint Joachim's proper-right arm and the illogical shadow projected by his proper-left hand on the table.

Although the artist generally painted directly over the *imprimatura*, he also painted specific areas in preparation for subsequent layers (the *bosquexo*, or undermodeling, as recommended by Pacheco in his treatise).[37] In the painting of Saint Anne's mantle, for example, the artist started with a solidly modeled *bosquexo*, using various shades of ochre, which was subsequently disregarded as it is only found in part of the mantle (fig. 14). The right side of the mantle was painted directly over the *imprimatura*. Saint Joachim's green garment, a mixture of azurite and yellow lake, was painted over a black layer that extends over most of the background.[38] His face, however, is painted directly over the *imprimatura*, which most likely means that the figure was part of the composition from the start. The presence of a black underlayer for the green garment seems to reflect a deliberate aesthetic decision rather than a change in the composition during the painting; the use of black underlayers was a common technical resource in tenebrist art, as the black layer below optically strengthened the luminosity of the lighter layer on top. The dog is also painted over a black paint layer covering the *imprimatura*. This too seems to be deliberate, as the shape for the cat, right next to the dog, appears to have been left in reserve and is painted directly over the *imprimatura*. Some white passages in the composition also have a fully modeled gray underlayer. This is the case, for instance, in the white plate, part of Saint Anne's headscarf, and the book, though no gray underlayer has been detected in the bundle of white cloth at the bottom-right corner.

The technique of the Yale painting does not seem particularly consistent or methodical.[39] As described earlier, there are numerous incongruities in the layer buildup, which no doubt relate to the artist changing his mind, and there are also large overlaps of elements that seem deliberate, such as that of the hands and the book over the figures' garments in the center of the composition or, on a smaller scale, the painting of the Virgin's index finger over that of her mother (see fig. 9).[40] However, there are also other areas—such as the table frame and the drawer at the left in the painting, the green drapery and the chair at the right, and even the cat and the dog in the foreground—that

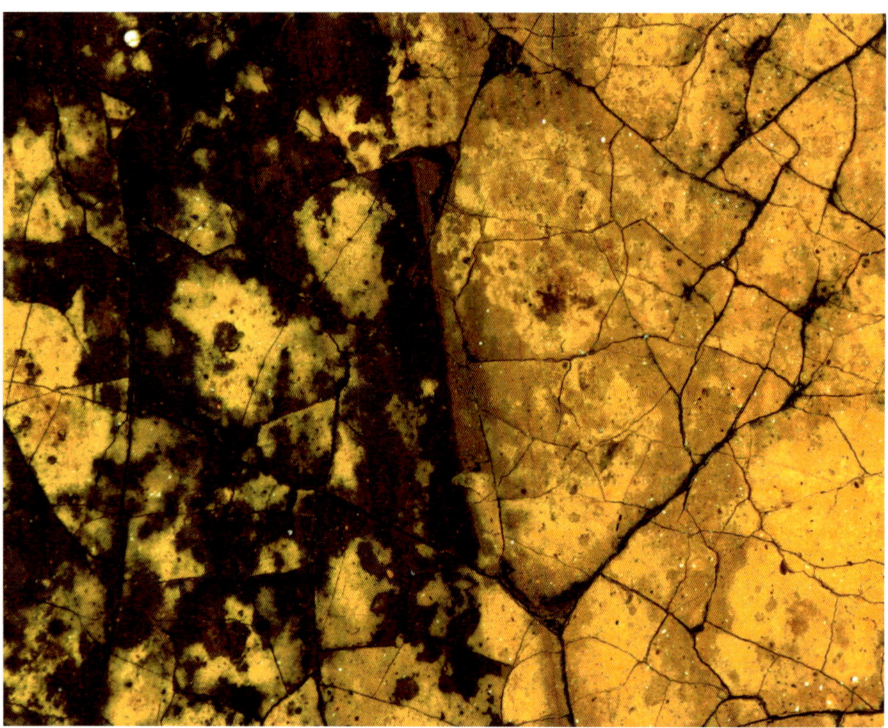

Fig. 14. Photomicrograph of the partial *bosquexo* (undermodeling) layer of the *Education of the Virgin*, visible through abrasion of the upper paint layers on the left of Saint Anne's ochre mantle

seem to have been painted with great care, with barely any modification in the original outline or overlapping of colors.

In conclusion, the results of the technical examination indicate that the *Education of the Virgin* shares many features with paintings from Velázquez's Sevillian period, especially in the choice of materials, the laying-in of the composition, and the handling of the paint layers. Not all of Velázquez's paintings from this period have been subjected to detailed technical examination and analysis, and further analogies might yet be found. The unusual number of changes in the painting, although not without parallel,[41] most likely reflects the hesitant approach of a very young but highly talented artist responding to the demands of one of his first major commissions—if not the very first of these—after completing his apprenticeship with Francisco Pacheco.

1. By comparison, the *Education of the Virgin* by Juan de Roelas (pl. 2) measures 230 × 170 cm. The closest painting in size from Velázquez's Sevillian period is his *Adoration of the Magi* (Museo Nacional del Prado, Madrid), at 203 × 125 cm.

2. Cusping is the undulating line of the canvas weave where it is pulled to a series of peaks by the fixing points at the edge of the canvas support. These lines are most marked at the original edge of the canvas.

3. For a short list of cleaning materials and methods from this period, see Massing 2012, 137.

4. For more information on Bradley, see his obituary on "The Distribution List," CoOL (Conservation OnLine), http://cool.conservation-us.org/byform//mailing-lists/cdl/instances/2004/2004-10-14.dst, posted October 11, 2004 (accessed February 10, 2014).

5. The material analysis was undertaken by Henry DePhillips, the Vernon Krieble Professor Emeritus of Chemistry, Trinity College, Hartford, Conn.

6. Marciari 2010.

7. The authors thank Emilio Botín, Executive Chairman, Salvador Medina, Global Director of Santander Universities, Global Division, and Eduardo Garrido, Director of Santander Universities, United States, all of Banco Santander, for their interest in and generous support of the project.

8. Carmen Albendea was appointed Associate Conservator of Paintings and assigned to the project in August 2012.

9. In the X-radiograph, the light spots indicate shaped pieces of old canvas of a similar weight to the original that were fitted into holes in the original fabric during the relining process.

10. This seems to be a feature of Velázquez's early paintings. When describing the X-radiograph of the *Portrait of a Young Man* (Museo Nacional del Prado, Madrid), Carmen Garrido Pérez, in Garrido Pérez 1992, 116, states that "la radiografía da una imagen del cuadro mucho más dinámica y detallista" ("the X-radiograph gives a much more dynamic and detailed image of the painting"; author's translation). Other authors who have noted this include Hale 2005, 75, and Zuccari, Véliz, and Fiedler 2005, 35–36.

11. Microscopic examination of the green curtain revealed the presence of a slightly translucent dark green layer over areas of a more opaque, lighter green, composed of blue (azurite) and yellow-lake pigments. This translucent layer appears to have darkened substantially, causing the loss of modeling in the drapery. The darkest shadows in this passage are achieved by painting the dark green directly over the dark *imprimatura*. Microscopic examination of a cross-section sample from the green curtain confirmed this, revealing a thin, brown-green top layer over the brighter green main paint layer. Elemental mapping of the green layers (using scanning electron microscopy and energy dispersive X-ray spectroscopy, or SEM-EDS) suggests that the darker top layer has more organic material relative to the brighter green layer. This may mean that the artist mixed more oil with the pigments to achieve a more transparent layer, but it is also possible that the top layer contains some copper resinate (a transparent green glaze produced using verdigris and natural resins) in addition to the mixture of azurite and yellow lake pigments.

12. *Mantelillo veneciano* is a relatively modern term and reflects Venetian artists' early use of the fabric as a painting support. However, in Spanish sixteenth- and seventeenth-century documentary sources, the terms *mantel* (tablecloth) and *mantel alimanisco* (tablecloth of German origin) are generally used; see Bruquetas Galán 2002, 237.

13. Paintings by Velázquez on a *mantelillo* support include the *Adoration of the Magi* and the *Venerable Mother Jerónima de la Fuente* (Museo Nacional del Prado, Madrid; see Garrido Pérez 1992, 75); *Portrait of Don Cristóbal Suárez de Ribera* (Museo de Bellas Artes de Sevilla; unpublished but noted in an X-radiograph kindly supplied by the museum); *Saint Ildefonso Receiving the Chasuble from the Virgin* (pl. 4; see Garrido Pérez 1992, 108); and the *Supper at Emmaus* (Metropolitan Museum of Art, New York; see Hale 2005, 70). It was also used in *Saint John in the Wilderness* (Art Institute of Chicago; see Zuccari, Véliz, and Fiedler 2005, 33), a work not universally accepted to be by Velázquez.

14. Véliz 1996, 79.

15. The presence of dolomite was inferred from SEM-EDS elemental analysis results and then verified using Raman spectroscopy on a polished paint cross section. Dolomite has been detected in

the grounds of other paintings from Velázquez's
Sevillian period, such as the *Adoration of the Magi*
and the *Venerable Mother Jerónima de la Fuente* (Museo
Nacional del Prado, Madrid; see McKim-Smith and
Newman 1993, 130); *Kitchen Scene with Christ in the House
of Martha and Mary* (Marciari, fig. 6; see Zuccari, Véliz,
and Fiedler 2005, 107n23); *Kitchen Scene* and *Portrait
of Góngora* (Art Institute of Chicago and Museum of
Fine Arts, Boston, respectively; see McKim-Smith
et al. 2005, 91); as well as in the grounds of several
other seventeenth- and eighteenth-century Sevillian
paintings (see Illán Gutiérrez, Romero Asenjo, and
Sáenz de Tejada 2005, 3). Rocío Bruquetas Galán
also makes reference to the presence of dolomite in
Velázquez's Sevillian grounds; see Bruquetas Galán
2002, 313. In addition to dolomite, elemental mapping
of cross sections located several elongated particles
containing aluminum, silicon, and potassium in the
ground. These probably represent cross sections of
platelike mica particles, which have been reported
as components of the ground layer in other early
Velázquez works. See McKim-Smith and Newman
1993, 130; Bruquetas Galán 2002, 313; and McKim-
Smith et al. 2005, 91. Analysis of the lead white was
performed on polished paint cross sections by SEM-
EDS. The ground is heterogeneous both in terms of
composition, since it is made up of multiple distinct
phases, and in terms of particle size, as the silica and
calcium carbonate particles appear to be quite coarse
compared to the other components.

16. See Pacheco 1990, 481.

17. *Venerable Mother Jerónima de la Fuente* (private collection,
thought to be an autograph replica of the Museo
Nacional del Prado version from about 1620) and
Portrait of a Young Man, ca. 1623 (Museo Nacional
del Prado, Madrid); see Garrido Pérez 1992, 95,
117. McKim-Smith and Newman 1993, 131, also
report the presence of a double preparation in the
Portrait of Francisco Pacheco(?) (Museo Nacional del
Prado, Madrid), dated 1619–22. A good number of
Velázquez's Sevillian paintings have yet to receive a
detailed technical examination, many of which might
have similar grounds. The variation in the method of
preparing the fabric supports in one artist's production could also be due to the artist using prepared
canvases from specialized workshops. See Bruquetas
Galán 2002, 314; and Gayo and Jover de Celis 2010, 47.

18. Elemental analysis was carried out on polished paint
cross sections using SEM-EDS. Garrido Pérez
1992, 86, reports the presence of "pequeños cristales
azules" (small blue glasslike particles) in the ground
of Velázquez's *Venerable Mother Jerónima de la Fuente* at
the Museo Nacional del Prado, Madrid.

19. For a reference to El Greco's use of palette scrapings of very similar composition for the *imprimatura*
layer, see Gayo and Jover de Celis 2010, 42–44.

20. According to Keith and Carr 2009, 52, although
Velázquez occasionally left the ground exposed in
the finished painting in some of his early works
(e.g., the *Immaculate Conception* and *Saint John the
Evangelist in the Island of Patmos*, both National Gallery,
London), this was done only for a few isolated
details, making it the exception rather than the rule.
McKim-Smith and Newman 1993, 113, also note
that Velázquez rarely left the ground visible in the
painting stage, in both his Sevillian and later works.

21. Blanching is an opaque whitening of a surface,
caused by the leaching out of some components in
the material and/or the development of a system
of cracks and fissures that scatter light, producing
a whitening effect. The blanching of Sevillian
grounds has been discussed by Véliz 1996, 80; Hale
2005, 76; and Keith 2006, 74.

22. See Véliz 1996, 80. Several other conservators
and art historians have since identified these
lines in some of Velázquez's early paintings. See
McKim-Smith 1999, 114; Hale 2005, 72; McKim-
Smith et al. 2005, 82; Zuccari, Véliz, and Fiedler
2005, 36; and Keith 2006, 72, 88. More recent
technical examination of paintings by Spanish
artists contemporary to Velázquez has revealed
that these lines were not only used by Velázquez
(see Zuccari, Véliz, and Fiedler 2005, 36): similar
lines have been detected in works by Alonso Cano,
Francisco Herrera the Elder, Jusepe Leonardo,
Francisco Pacheco, Luis Tristán, and Francisco
Zurbarán. In Zuccari, Véliz, and Fiedler 2005,
40, the authors state, "What is distinctive about
Velázquez's use of this technique is the boldness,
precision, fluidity, and X-ray opacity of the lines
and contours." In a recent communication with
Zahira Véliz, she confirmed that X-radio-opaque
lines have recently been detected in works by
Velázquez's contemporaries.

23. Depending on the thickness of these lines, they can sometimes be discerned in raking light.

24. One of these lines (the red line on Virgin's shoulder) appears to lie on top of black underpaint, although it is unclear whether this black paint is part of the background or one of the brushy underdrawing lines applied prior to painting.

25. This was determined using thermally assisted hydrolysis and methylation gas chromatography mass spectrometry on a sample taken from the green curtain in the upper-right quadrant. On drying oils in Spanish seventeenth-century works, see Bruquetas Galán 2002, 324. According to that author, the two most common drying oils in Spanish seventeenth-century paintings were linseed oil and walnut oil. The first was more compact and had better drying properties; the second yellowed less, which is why it was used for whites, blues, and flesh tones. However, Pacheco preferred to use purified linseed oil for these colors.

26. Analysis was performed using in situ nondestructive X-ray fluorescence spectroscopy (XRF) as well as SEM-EDS analysis of polished cross-section samples. Raman spectroscopy was also used to study components in cross sections. Fourier-transform infrared spectroscopy (FTIR) was used to characterize unmounted paint-sample fragments.

27. XRF analysis detected manganese in addition to iron in the dark foreground, suggesting the use of umber. The use of umber can also be inferred in the shaded folds of Saint Anne's yellow drapery.

28. The artist's use of bone black can be inferred from the detection of phosphorous in XRF spectra collected from the dark foreground. SEM-EDS verified the presence of phosphorus and calcium in dark particles within the top layer of the dark foreground as well as in the green top layer of a cross section from Saint Joachim's robe.

29. Lead white is present throughout the top paint layers and, in low amounts, in the ground and *imprimatura* layers.

30. XRF analysis indicates an almost exclusive use of yellow ochre for the yellow passages. Yellow ochre areas have a high proportion of transparent, angular particles that vary in size and some of which are very coarse. Elemental mapping (using SEM-EDS) indicated the presence of a high proportion of silica particles mixed with yellow ochre in Saint Anne's robe and also located multiple large silica particles in an ochre layer under the angel's light blue garment. The angular silica particles are also prominent in the ground. Areas of "pitting" throughout the painting surface (particularly noticeable in the ochre passages) seem to be caused by some of these protruding particles being swept off during previous abrasive cleanings. The yellow ochre passages also contain a considerable amount of deep brown translucent particles that are yet to be identified.

31. Red lake was used primarily for the Virgin's robe but also as a component of other paint passages. The substrate of the red lake appears to contain aluminum, based on XRF analysis.

32. The azurite particles generally appear to be very finely ground, which may account to some degree for the dull appearance of Saint Anne's blue garment.

33. Azurite was detected in this area based on visual examination under a stereomicroscope. However, examination of a paint cross-section sample, using reflected light microscopy and SEM-EDS, revealed that the azurite particles were only present in the *imprimatura* layer and smalt was only present in the top layer.

34. The tin and lead were detected by XRF analysis.

35. Garrido Pérez 1992, 125.

36. One of Velázquez's working practices in his early paintings (and which he continued to employ throughout most of his painting career) is the application of random brush marks during the painting process to either test the color of the paint or to discharge the brush. Although these brush wipings were covered by the final paint layers, they sometimes become visible to the naked eye due to the increase in the transparency of the paint layers over time. However, in most cases, X-radiography and infrared imaging techniques are needed to document their presence.

37. Pacheco 1990, 482.

38. The use of azurite and yellow lake is consistent with Velázquez's practice for green passages, as he rarely used green pigments, preferring different mixtures of blue and yellow, as noted by Garrido Pérez 1992, 24; McKim-Smith and Newman 1993, 124; McKim-Smith 1999, 115; Hale 2005, 72; McKim-Smith et al. 2005, 91; Zuccari, Véliz, and Fiedler

2005, 34–35; and Keith 2006, 88n34. Visual examination of cross sections indicated the presence of blue
and bluish-green particles in a moss-green matrix.
Elemental mapping of green paint layers detected
copper in the location of the blue particles, which
likely indicates the use of azurite. The moss-green
matrix consists of finely divided calcium-containing
particles, which most likely represent the calcium
carbonate substrate of a yellow organic plant-based
dye, such as weld or dyer's broom. Samples of green
paint layers were analyzed using FTIR spectroscopy,
which confirmed the presence of azurite as well as
calcium carbonate, in the form of calcite.

39. This lack of consistency seems to reflect Carmen
Garrido Pérez's summary of Velázquez's technique
when she states in Garrido Pérez 1992, 20, that "en
líneas generales hay que resaltar que, a primera vista,
su técnica no resulta muy cuidada, en el sentido
tradicional del término. El pintor no está preocu-
pado por los academicismos de épocas anteriores,
ni puede decirse que respete con fidelidad los
recetarios pictóricos que tanto preocuparon a su
suegro" (in general terms, it needs to be noted that
the first impression of his technique is that it is
not very meticulous, in the traditional sense of the
term. The artist was not worried about the canons
of academic art, and one cannot say that he was
always respectful of the pictorial recipe books that
his father-in-law was so concerned about; author's
translation). Already in 1979, Gridley McKim-Smith
also emphasized Velázquez's lack of consistency in
his working method; see McKim-Smith 1979, 603.

40. Saint Anne's index finger was painted before that of
the Virgin, even though it might seem the opposite
when this area is looked at with the naked eye, due
to the abrasion of the Virgin's finger (much more
thinly painted), which makes it appear as if Saint
Anne's finger was in front.

41. The X-radiograph of Velázquez's *Waterseller of Seville*
(Apsley House, London), reveals that the boy was
originally holding a bottle or jug in his proper-right
hand, before the artist painted this out and moved
the boy's hand so that his forefinger crooks around
the stem of the glass held by the waterseller. We
are grateful to Rachel Turnbull, Senior Collections
Conservator, English Heritage, United Kingdom,
for providing access to the X-radiograph.

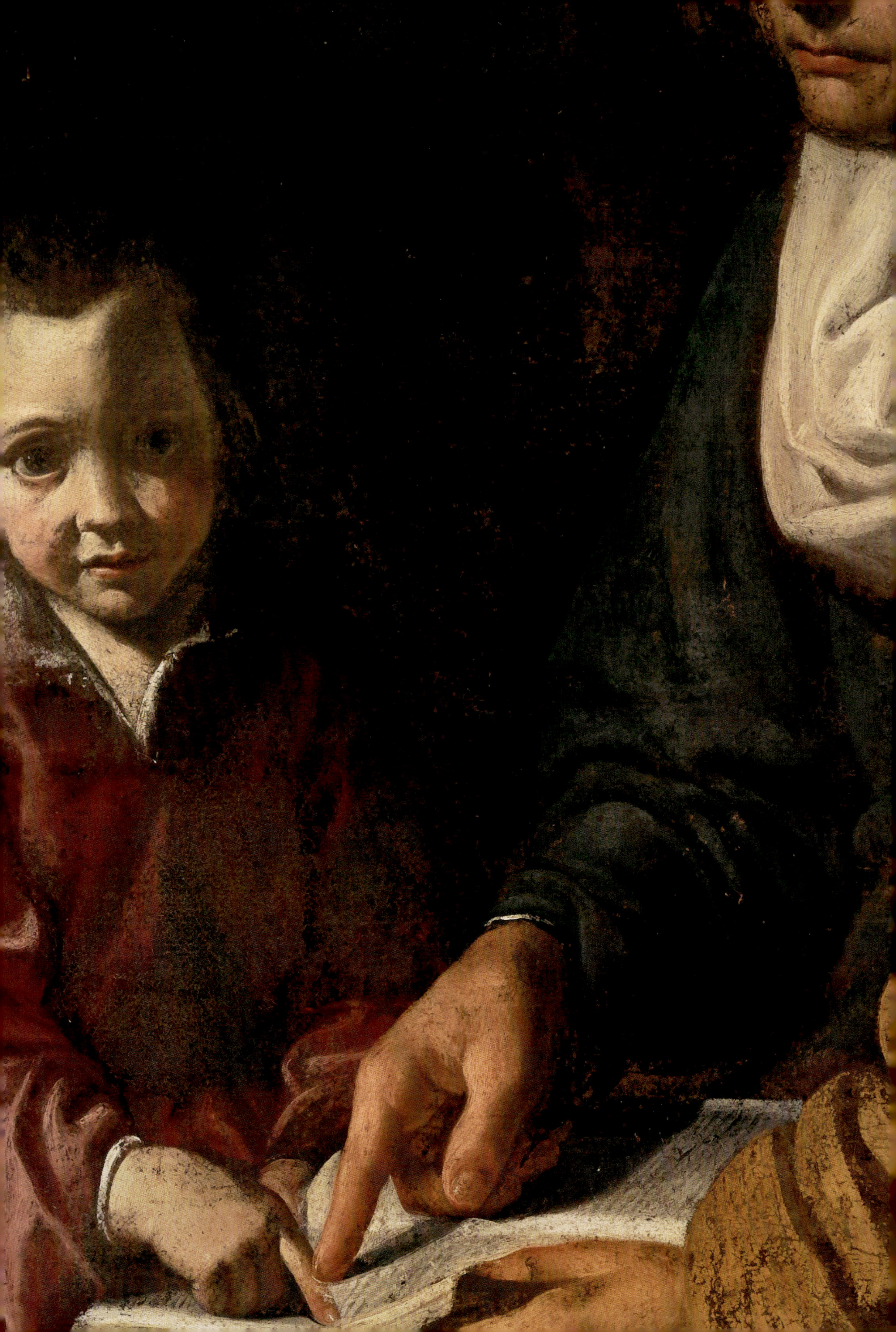

THE EDUCATION OF THE VIRGIN AND THE SHAPING OF EARLY NATURALISM

BENITO NAVARRETE PRIETO

When Diego Velázquez began his training as an apprentice in the workshop of Francisco Pacheco on September 27, 1611, an assortment of circumstances would have led him to associate himself with one of the most influential personalities of Seville. The modernity of Pacheco's painting would not have been one of them, but they certainly would have included Pacheco's connections with the intellectual and cultural elites of the city,[1] not to mention his work as a practical instructor in the artisanal recipes and procedures of the art of painting. It should not be overlooked that the young Velázquez had previously studied with Francisco Herrera the Elder—an artist who, judging by his first known works, which date from 1614 and 1615, had become mired in a backward-looking and artificial mannerism by the early 1610s.

Nevertheless, Velázquez's training with Pacheco shines a light on and fuels one of the most common themes in artistic historiography, namely that of the young artist who, with his genius and innate talent, surpasses the master. But despite Velázquez's inherent abilities, for this eclipse to occur a few special qualities were necessary, ones that would facilitate his absorption and transformation of the innovations then being brought forth by the most modern artists of the day.

Thus Velázquez came to manifest his talent by attending to the lessons of those artists who were active in Seville in the previous century,[2] as well as by paying close attention to those who were able to transform themselves into innovators in Sevillian painting and those who were blazing a new direction for Spanish painting. The period from 1600 to 1620 was a crucial one in art history, during which radical changes occurred that led painters to turn toward painting from life. Considering both works that have long been known and those newly coming to light, there can be no doubt that Velázquez was the real protagonist of this change.

This is the reason why the present author considers the Yale University Art Gallery's *Education of the Virgin* (pl. 1) to be a work of paramount importance from this period—precisely because it is evidence of the crystalization of a series of formulas that make it unique in its genre, and because it is probably the first painting in which Velázquez began to experiment with the formulas that led him to give concrete form to his interest in nature and the reality of his surroundings; these formulas were soon revealed in other paintings he created in Seville before 1624, the year he set off for the court.[3] Schooled in the assimilation of reformed mannerism, Velázquez had an awareness of the contributions of those artists who had timidly approached the representation of lived and felt reality.[4] The Yale canvas is clear testimony to that incipient apprenticeship and the first brilliant manifestation of characteristics that were to become consubstantial in Velázquez's painting: the triumph of the gestural, the monumentality of physical presence, and the study of human passion as the mirror of the soul, as well as the sense of space and the profoundly intimate and familiar atmosphere.

At the same time, the painting is evidence of the impact on the young artist of the reference points presented in the exhibition *De Herrera a Velázquez: El primer naturalismo en Sevilla*:[5] the Romanism of Pablo de Céspedes, the compositional schemes of Juan de Roelas, and the physical types and flowing draperies of Luis Tristán. To understand how much of these artists there is in the *Education of the Virgin*, it is necessary to compare the painting with three works: the *Holy Family* by Céspedes (fig. 1), which was painted around 1592 and, until a few years ago, was in the vestuary of the Beneficiados of the cathedral of Seville; the *Education of the Virgin* by Roelas, from around 1612 (pl. 2), originally in the Merced Calzada convent in Seville and now in the Museo de Bellas Artes in that city; and, finally, the *Holy Family* signed in 1613 by Luis Tristán and now preserved in the Minneapolis Institute of Arts (pl. 3). All three were painted just before Velázquez's apprenticeship with Pacheco concluded and exemplify the work of reformed mannerists who were showing early signs of naturalism in their art.[6]

Velázquez's own master, as Pacheco's discussion of the artist in his *Arte de la pintura* illustrates, was aware that Velázquez had chosen the path of painting from life, though there is a question as to whether Pacheco was aware of his future son-in-law's genius, precocity, and modernity from the moment he began to instruct him in his workshop. At exactly the time that Velázquez was serving his apprenticeship, Pacheco was embarking on some of the most important works of his career: the *Last Judgment* for the church of the convent of Santa Isabel, executed between 1611 and 1614, and the

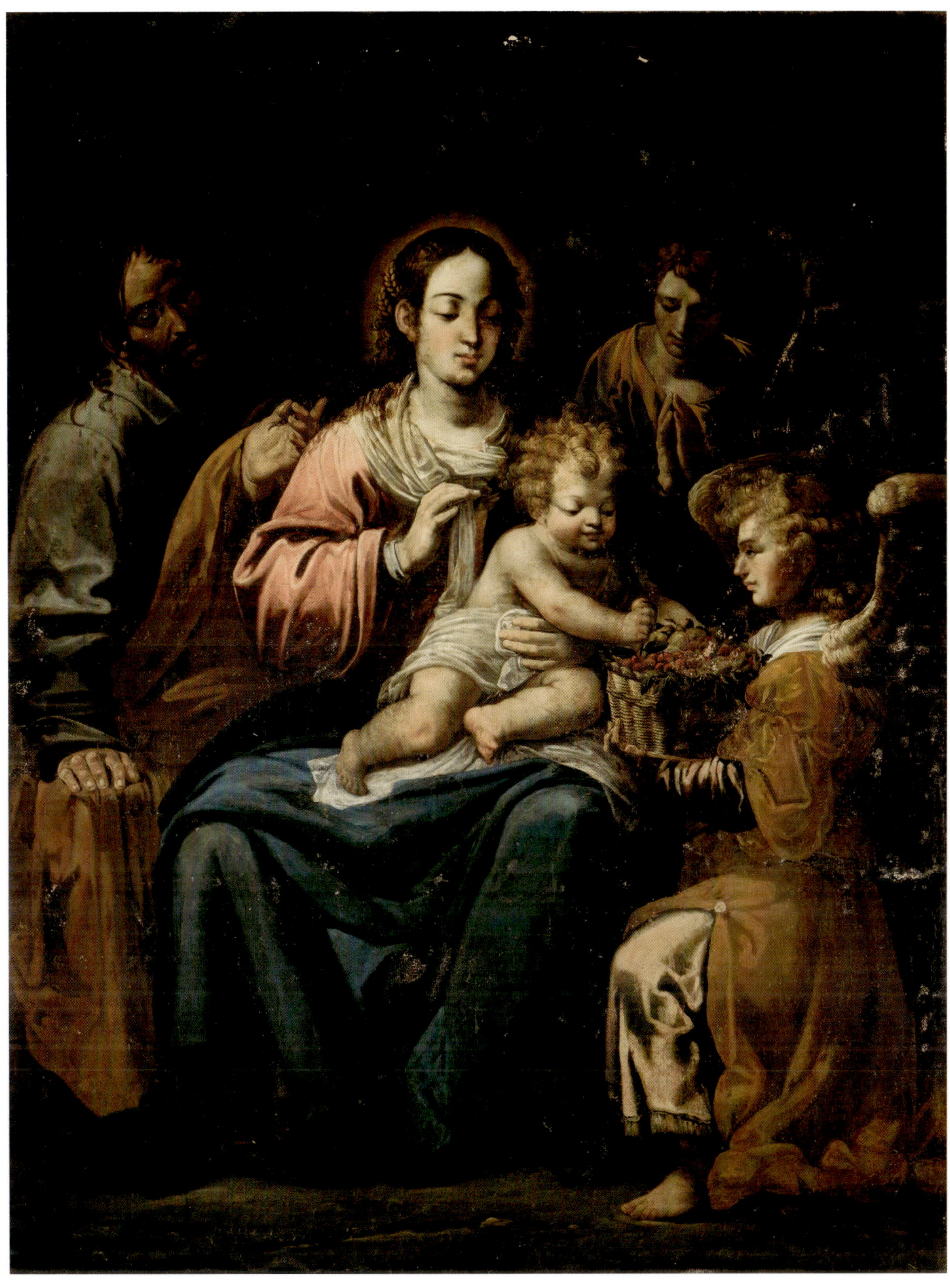

Fig. 1. Pablo de Céspedes, *The Holy Family*, ca. 1592. Oil on canvas, 188 × 146 cm (74 × 57¼ in.). Cathedral of Santa María de la Sede, Seville

Christ Served by the Angels for the refectory of the convent of San Clemente, painted between 1615 and 1616, both now in the Musée Goya in Castres, France. Probably the best of his output can be seen in these works. It may thus be necessary to speak of what the one artist owes to the other and, as Jean Louis Augé suggests, of a possible transmission instead of a transgression.[7]

What did the pupil gain from the master, and what did the pupil impart? This is a question that could apply equally to Velázquez and Herrera the Elder. Beginning in the 1620s—and especially when he undertook his ensemble dedicated to the life of Saint Bonaventure in 1628—Herrera the Elder adopted the naturalist formulas seen in Velázquez's painting, which could lead to the conclusion that the two old masters wound up being attracted to the path that their revolutionary young disciple had taken.

Velázquez had probably begun the *Education of the Virgin* around 1615–17, when he had not yet passed the examination that would make him a master painter. He did not hesitate to look to the Roman monumentality in the aforementioned *Holy Family* by Céspedes, which was painted toward the end of the sixteenth century, and to reinterpret the close, intimate atmosphere of that painting, as well as its coloration and impasto, the fluidity of its brushstrokes, and its strongly realistic details, such as the face of Saint Joseph.[8] Nevertheless, Velázquez was more under the sway of the revolutionary figure of Roelas and the modernity that dwelt in Roelas's painting, which really should be considered the crucible in which naturalist forms materialized in Spanish painting.[9] On the other hand, a comparison between these two artists' different ways of approaching the *Education of the Virgin,* and theoretical analysis of the works in light of what Pacheco says in *Arte de la pintura* about Velázquez's desire to paint from life, can aid in comprehending the true essence and importance of the Yale painting. To begin with, it would unquestionably be necessary to banish the erroneous belief, long held by art historians, that the Roelas painting had a Venetian affiliation. On the contrary, his painting is much better understood in the context of Flemish art; Flanders was one of the pathways through which naturalism first began to enter into painting in Seville, and it must be remembered that Roelas was really a Flemish painter.[10] The Flemish influence can be noted in both Roelas's technique and his colors and forms, and along with the deep-rooted Caravaggesque influences of Tristán, it was of overriding significance for Velázquez, as the work under study here shows.

Still, the *Education of the Virgin* is also a painting that made use of a theme clearly rooted in the Middle Ages and a particularly domestic and feminine subject, one that favored the spread of the iconography of Saint Anne as a teacher.[11] Together with the subject of the Holy Family, it was used by artists as a pretext for emphasizing everyday reality, and it was especially disseminated and patronized by the Carmelite order.[12] Roelas was the first to broach it on canvas in Seville, but he took as his point of departure an earlier sculptural model, mentioned by Pacheco in his *Arte de la pintura*, that really solidified the guidelines for this iconography, not only because of Pacheco's reference to it but also because it was recommended as an archetype to be followed in certain contractual documents. It thus continues to be of interest that when Pacheco spoke critically of this iconography in his *Arte de la pintura*, he indicated—basing his remarks, as he says, on the apocryphal gospels—that:

> with less foundation and greater frequency, artists today depict the blessed Saint Anne teaching the Mother of God to read, a new subject, but one embraced by the vulgar. I say new, because it is about twenty-four years, more or less, from the time it began down to 1636, when a sculpture of Saint Anne in a chapel at the parochial church of the Magdalena was given by a modern sculptor an accompanying sculpture of the young Virgin reading; from there, run-of-the-mill painters have propagated it, to the point where the licentiate Juan de Roelas (skillful in coloring, though lacking in decoration) has dignified it with his brush, in the convent of Merced in this City.[13]

Thus the model Roelas followed was probably a sculpture from the sixteenth century to which the child Virgin was later added, and which was venerated in the defunct church of the Magdalena and, unfortunately, has not survived. A 1678 document shows that this sculpture was a known and reputable example of this artistic iconography in Seville; in the document, the comissioner, Andrés Barba de Figueroa, charges Francisco Antonio Ruiz Gijón with creating a sculpture for the sacrament chapel of the collegiate church of Olivares, in the province of Seville, describing the commission as:

> an image from life of the Lady Saint Anne seated on a chair and of our lady at an early age together with her holy mother, as she is teaching her to read, placed over a small platform, in the same way as another work similar to this in the church of the Magdalena in this city, in the chapel next to the blessed Christ carrying the cross.[14]

As the sculpture by Gijón for Olivares has been preserved (fig. 2), it is possible to corroborate that, as Pacheco indicated, Roelas relied on it as a model, and that Velázquez's painting undoubtedly must also be related to it, as he was inspired by Roelas's ensemble. The analogy is important for demonstrating the interaction that existed between painting and sculpture,[15] since the latter form displayed the recommended iconography from

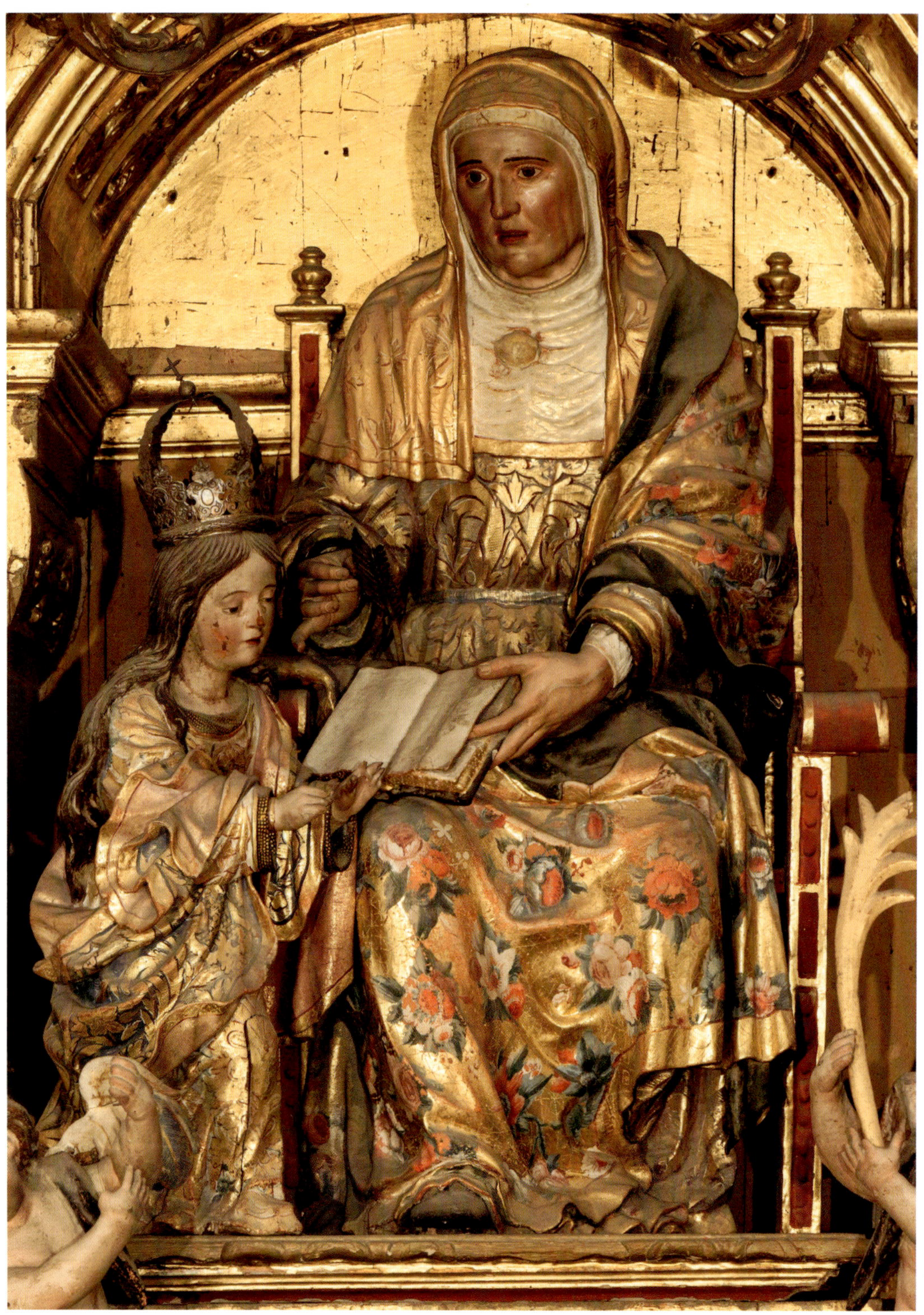

Fig. 2. Francisco Antonio Ruiz Gijón, *Saint Anne Teaching the Virgin to Read*, from the top of the altarpiece in the chapel of the Sacraments, 1678. Polychromed wood, dimensions unknown. Colegiata de Santa María de las Nieves, Olivares, Seville

which artists took their point of departure, naturalizing and adapting it to their own different styles.[16] Comparison of the Gijón sculpture with the two pictorial interpretations further helps to highlight both the assimilation of Roelas and the modernity of Velázquez. There is a key element shared by the three works of art: the volume and solidity of the body of the seated Saint Anne. Yet while Roelas inverts the position of the saint, Velázquez places her in the same position as in the sculpture, with a gravity and solidity that are reminiscent of the Romanism of Céspedes, as well as of the sculpture itself. Perhaps the greatest similarity between the sculpture and Velázquez's work is the way in which Saint Anne holds the book and inserts a finger into it to mark her place.

A comparison of the way in which Roelas and Velázquez interpret this scene facilitates an understanding of how much separates the one artist from the other and explains Velázquez's transition from a reformed mannerist to an artist who was decidedly practicing naturalism. While the Roelas painting shows the attitude of the child Virgin as one of a pupil pointing to and learning the sacred scriptures with a certain doubtful hesitancy (pl. 2), Velázquez's work transforms her attitude into one of steadiness, sureness, and firmness (pl. 1). In his treatise, Pacheco mentions what Saint Anselm and Saint Epiphanius had affirmed: that the Virgin acquired her learning through knowledge bestowed by the grace of God. This is Velázquez's diametrically opposed and radical way of presenting the Virgin. Docile and with bowed head in the Roelas painting, in the Velázquez she is seen standing straight and looking fixedly at the viewer, not the book. There is a profound difference in conception here—the difference between an old master who was making advances in coloration and composition and a young genius who was assimilating the grandeur of theoretical underpinnings and, by presenting the Virgin as wise by her very nature, transcending them in a natural and realistic way.

The two works deal with the protagonists' character and situation in space in opposite ways. In the Roelas work, space is established as an accommodation for the objects and figures, while in the Velázquez, it is the figures and forms that construct the space as the light falls on them. The wisdom of Velázquez's composition and of the way in which he illuminates the protagonists makes clear, more than ever, the precocious genius of the young painter—a genius that no one else in the first third of the seventeenth century could have been able to express.

Nevertheless, the Roelas work displays a feature that evidently was picked up by Velázquez: the realistic way in which some of the faces of the characters are modeled. This quality began to appear in the faces of Roelas's *Liberation of Saint Peter*, dated 1612 (fig. 3), which, together with Tristán's forms, succeeded in bringing about the triumph of a naturalist physiognomy in painting. As Acisclo Antonio Palomino affirmed,

[T]he paintings that achieved the greatest harmony in [Velázquez's] view were those of Luis Tristán (a disciple of Dominico Greco), a painter from Toledo, because they followed a course similar to his own humor, and because of how extraordinary the thinking and liveliness of the concepts was; and for this reason he declared himself to be his imitator, and ceased to follow the way of his master. . . . They gave [Velázquez] the name of a second Caravaggio, because he imitated nature so successfully in his works.[17]

The *Holy Family* in the Minneapolis Institute of Arts (pl. 3), signed and dated by Tristán in 1613, is probably the work that best represents Velázquez's intentions in the Yale painting. Tristán's painting should be understood as the culmination of the formulas the artist learned in Rome between 1607 and 1609, a period during which it has been possible to document that the artist was in the Eternal City.[18] In the painting, the presence of solutions similar to those employed by Orazio Borgianni and Carlo Saraceni is clear, above all in the detail of the dove and in the audacious treatment of the draperies, which are folded in great waves (fig. 4), as well as in the faces, such as the Virgin's (fig. 5). The Virgin's features

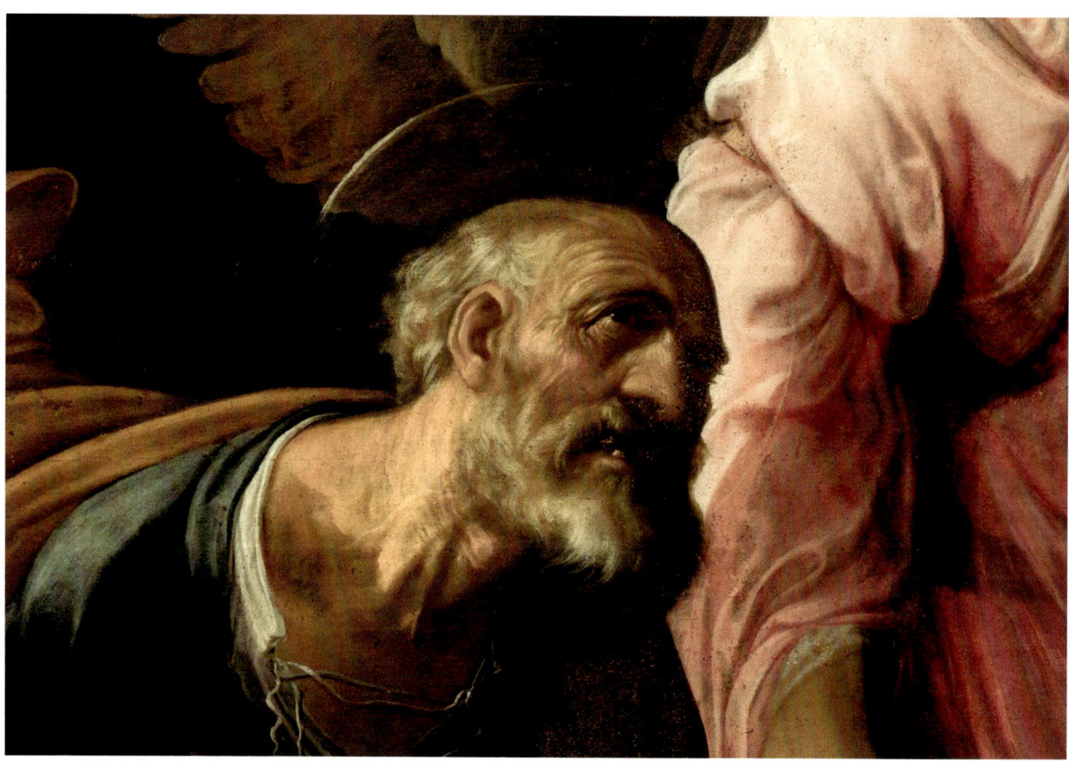

Fig. 3. Juan de Roelas, detail of the face of Saint Peter in the *Liberation of Saint Peter*, 1612. Oil on canvas, 305 × 207 cm (10 ft. 1/16 in. × 81 1/2 in.). Church of San Pedro, Seville

were soon reinterpreted by Velázquez in his *Immaculate Conception* in the National Gallery, London (see Marciari, fig. 8). Similarly, the wrinkled features of Saint Joachim in the Yale painting can easily be found in some of Tristán's versions of the *Tears of Saint Peter*, such as the one preserved in the National Museum of Poznan, Poland, or in the Palacio Real de Madrid. The intimacy that breathes throughout the scene in the Yale painting, the treatment of the lighting, and the attention to naturalist elements—such as the writing desk in the foreground, covered with a cloth on which a sewing basket with white linen can be seen, and the curtains that can be divined in the background—attest

to the pathway *caravaggismo* took to enter into Sevillian painting. It has been supposed that, just after his stay in Rome, Tristán passed through Seville, in 1611, which would account for the presence of his works there; his *Holy Family*, then, the first known work dated by the artist, stands forth as a model for understanding the forms that Velázquez began to develop in his *Education of the Virgin*—both in the contrasts of light and dark and in the intimate atmosphere he recreated, as well as in the monumental fall of the drapery.[19]

Apart from the connections to the Yale painting already established by Marciari in other canvases by Velázquez, such as the old man in the *Tavern Scene* in

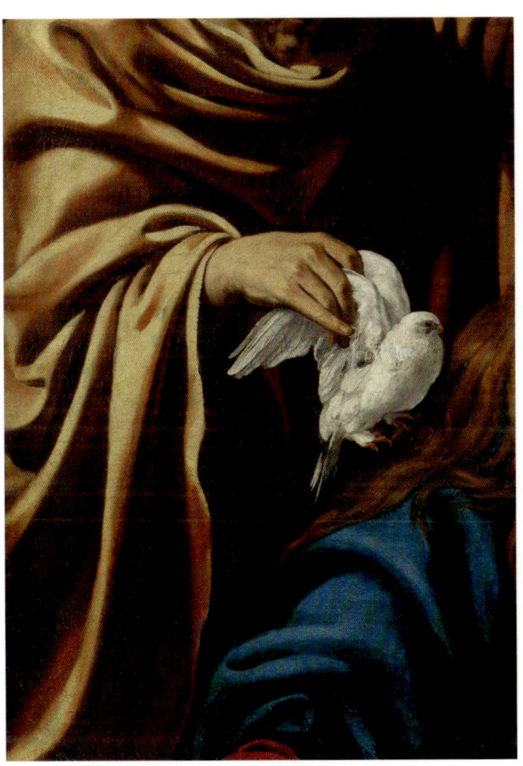

Fig. 4. Luis Tristán, detail of the dove and draperies in the *Holy Family* (pl. 3)

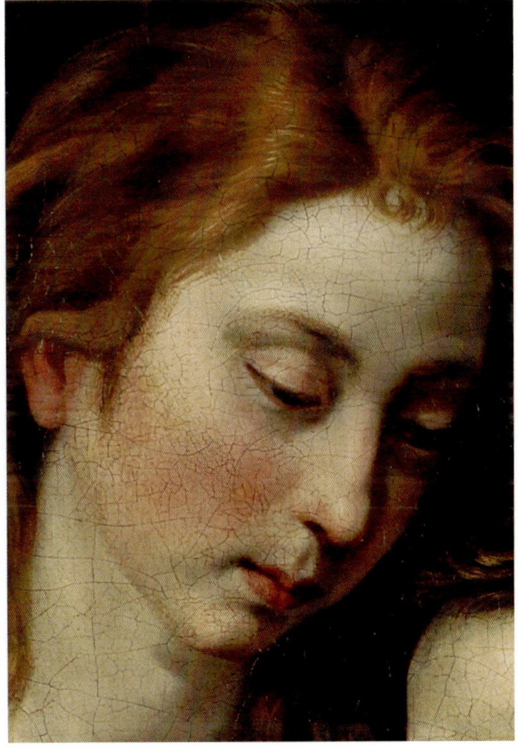

Fig. 5. Luis Tristán, detail of the Virgin in the *Holy Family* (pl. 3)

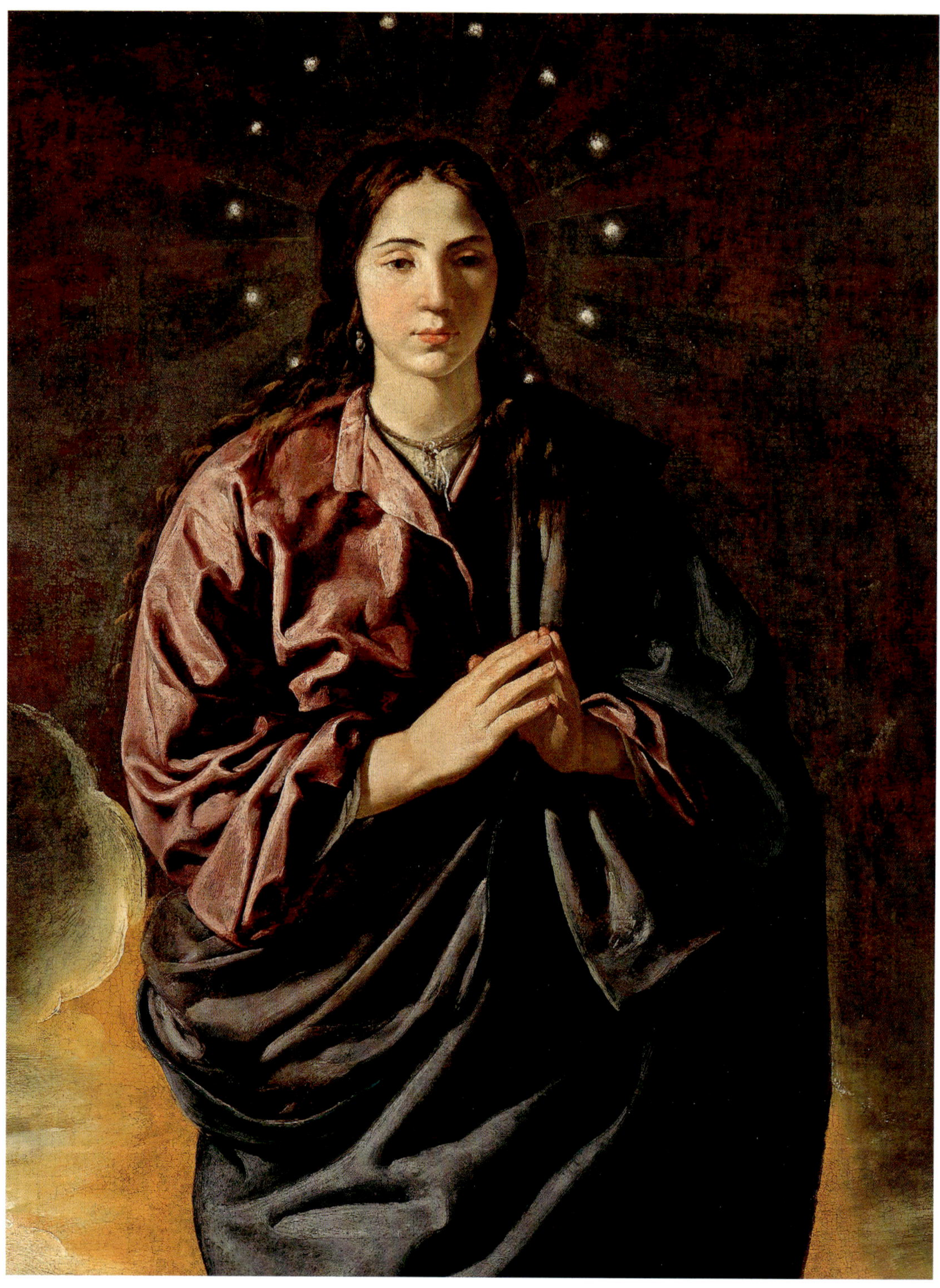

Fig. 6. Diego Velázquez, detail of the *Immaculate Conception*, ca. 1617. Oil on
canvas, 142 × 98.2 cm (55⅞ × 38⅝ in.). Fundación Focus-Abengoa, Seville

the Szépmüvészeti Múzeum, Budapest, and the drapery folds in the *Saint Thomas* in the Musée des Beaux-Arts d'Orléans (see Marciari, fig. 7), there is an indisputable relationship, both in the style and in the modeling of the rose-colored paint, between the sleeve of the child Virgin and that of the Virgin of the *Immaculate Conception* in the Fundación Focus-Abengoa, Seville (fig. 6), which, as has previously been argued, is also an early painting in the artist's oeuvre that should be dated, like the Yale painting, between 1616 and 1617.[20] A comparison of the sleeve of the Virgin in the *Immaculate Conception* with the X-radiograph of the sleeve and neck of the child Virgin in the *Education* (fig. 7) readily reveals in the folds a similarity in the fluidity of the pictorial *ductus*, which may even find its origins in the sleeve of the Virgin in the *Holy Family* by Céspedes in the cathedral of Seville (fig. 8). The paint in the *Immaculate Conception* is scrubbed rapidly across the surface, leaving a diluted tracing across the center and accumulated pigment at the edges.[21] The same technique can be seen in the better-preserved parts of the Yale painting, not only in the Virgin's sleeve but also in the angel's in the upper part of the canvas (fig. 9).

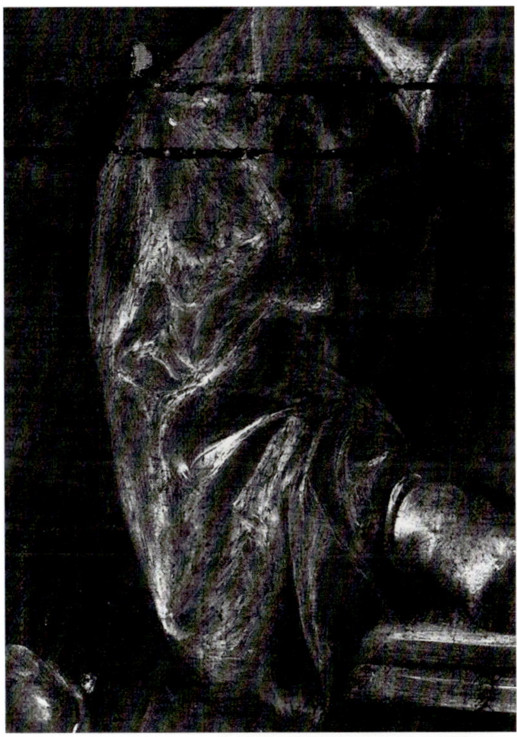

Fig. 7. Detail of the X-radiograph of the *Education of the Virgin*, showing the Virgin's sleeve

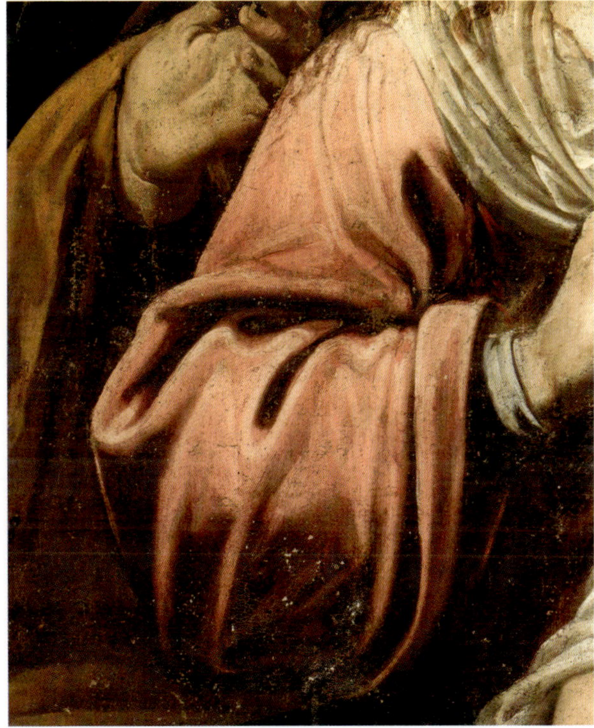

Fig. 8. Pablo de Céspedes, detail of the Virgin's sleeve in the *Holy Family*

The figure of the child Virgin with a penetrating and melancholy gaze is the precursor of experiments and ideas that would be developed and find acceptance in the future, making it evident how much Herrera the Elder owed to the young Velázquez. Curiously, in his maturity, the old master must have felt an attraction for the revolutionary forms of Velázquez, whose first creative ideas the elder painter had probably ignited—even before Pacheco's influence. Close observation of the figure of the child Saint John the Evangelist in Herrera the Elder's *Holy Family* in the Museo de Bellas Artes, Bilbao (fig. 10), which follows the pictorial sense of Velázquez's early work, seems to support this view.[22] The re-creation of earlier models would have been habitual in the painting of the first third of the seventeenth century, the period in which this work was made, giving a more naturalistic and realistic quality to fixed prototypes that began to repeat themselves in the artist's mind. In this way, Velázquez's repertory was configured based on forms he himself created; by observation of the real world; and through the suggestions of other, earlier forms brought forth by Céspedes, Roelas, and Tristán, painters who are key to understanding the evolution of the young artist's painting and the crystalization of naturalist formulas in his work—as is shown by the Yale *Education of the Virgin*, which now, happily, temporarily returns to Seville.

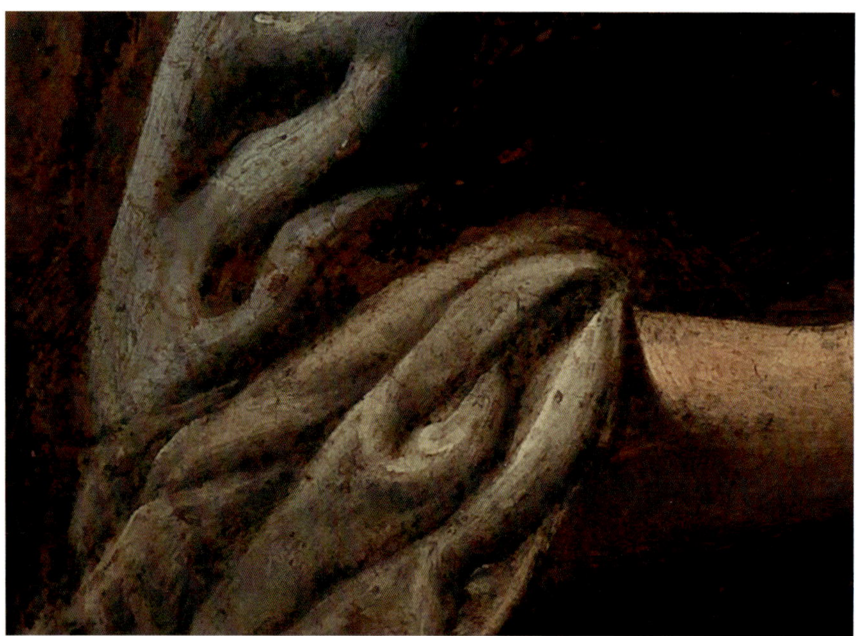

Fig. 9. Diego Velázquez, detail of the angel's sleeve in the *Education of the Virgin*

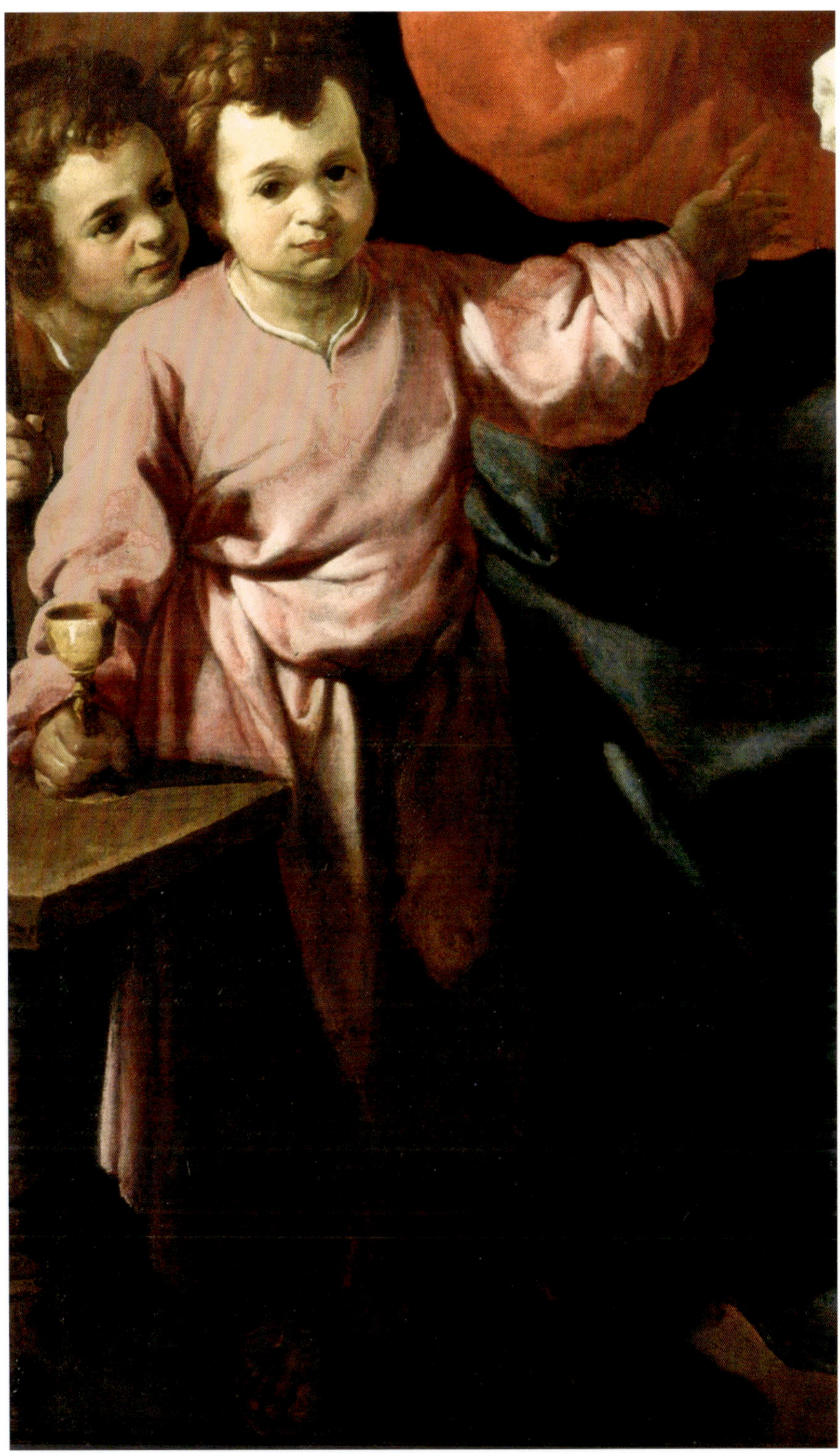

Fig. 10. Francisco Herrera the Elder, detail of the child Saint John the Evangelist in the *Holy Family*, ca. 1636–37. Oil on canvas, 194 × 177 cm (76⅜ × 69¹¹⁄₁₆ in.). Museo de Bellas Artes, Bilbao

The author is grateful to Jock Reynolds, Laurence Kanter, Ian McClure, and Carmen Albendea for providing the facilities to study this painting, and for their invaluable help in making it possible for it to be exhibited in Seville.

1. See Lleó Cañal 1996.

2. This is the thesis of Professor Juan Miguel Serrera in Serrera 1996, which also constituted the central thesis of the 1999 exhibition *Velázquez y Sevilla*; see Seville 1999.

3. For the relationships between the *Education of the Virgin* and other paintings from Velázquez's Sevillian period, see Marciari 2010, 150–51, and his essay "The Young Velázquez: *The Education of the Virgin*" in this catalogue. It is difficult to understand how, without setting forth a single formal, technical, or theoretical argument or rationale, this painting is ascribed to an anonymous Sevillian artist in a recent book by Tanya Tiffany; see Tiffany 2012, 10–11, fig. 5.

4. The term *reformed mannerist* was coined by Roberto Longhi and has come into favor for understanding those artists who began to depict an everyday and realistic atmosphere in their works; see Longhi 1951. The historian who has most successfully developed this concept and applied it to Spanish painting is Alfonso E. Pérez Sánchez; see Pérez Sánchez 1968.

5. Seville and Bilbao 2005–6.

6. It is interesting to note that at about this time Herrera the Elder continued to be mired in mannerist compositions that were more artificial than those of Roelas, as his 1615 *Mystical Betrothal of Saint Catherine*, in the Museo de Sevilla, reveals; for the *Mystical Betrothal*, see Navarrete Prieto 2007a, 252, fig. 6.

7. Augé 2007.

8. This painting was actually conceived as terminating in a middle point, probably because it formed part of an altarpiece; it acquired its present-day quadrangular format at an undetermined date. The painting was attributed to Céspedes by Juan Miguel Serrera; see Serrera 1984, 373, fig. 358. The author is grateful to Teresa Laguna for making it possible to photograph and study this painting.

9. For a new evaluation of Roelas's activity, see Seville 2008–9. See also the study dedicated to *Saint Anne Teaching the Virgin to Read* in Muñoz 2008, 170–71, cat. 24.

10. On Roelas's Flemish origins and his activities in Valladolid between 1598 and 1602, see Fernández del Hoyo 2000a and Fernández del Hoyo 2000b, 22–23.

11. On the iconography of Saint Anne in the Middle Ages, see Ashley and Sheingorn 1990; and Nixon 2004.

12. The provenance of the Yale painting is not really known, although John Marciari has speculated that it originated in the convent of Carmelite nuns of Santa Ana in Seville, for which Juan Martínez Montañés created a sculptural ensemble of the same subject, although with a very different conception, dated between 1627 and 1630, and still extant; see Marciari 2010, 151. Félix González de León describes what would seem to be the sculptural ensemble by Montañés, together with a Saint Joachim (now lost), on the main altarpiece of the church of the convent of Santa Ana: "El retablo mayor es de pésimo gusto y en un gran nicho que contiene en su centro, se venera a Sta Ana sentada, dando lección de leer a la Sma. Virgen niña, y al lado S. Joaquín, en pie" (The main altarpiece is in terrible taste and in a large niche contained in its center, St. Anne, seated and giving a lesson to the most holy Virgin as a child, is venerated alongside a standing St. Joachim; author's translation). This description coincides with the subject of the Yale painting; see González de León 1844, 173. On the other hand, Antonio Ponz cites "a *Saint Anne Teaching the Virgin to Read* by Alonso Cano in a dark chapel within the church [of the convent of San José], which I could not see well"; this church belongs to the discalced Mercedarians in Seville. The painting has been linked by some authors with the one attributed to Cano that was in the Benavites collection and later in the collection of the marquess of Espeja; see Ponz 1947, 790. See also Martínez Chumillas 1948, 164, fig. 105. Nevertheless, Harold Wethey does not connect the Benavites/Espeja work with the aforementioned one in the church of San José; see Wethey 1955, 157, fig. 164. The present author believes that this latter citation should be borne in mind regarding this painting, since Ponz could actually have been

referring to a work from Cano's Sevillian period rather than his Granadan period, and confusing it with a work by Velázquez, as has occurred on so many occasions.

13. Pacheco 1990, 582–83.

14. See Hernández Díaz 1928, 219. The author is grateful to Professor José Roda Peña, of the Universidad de Sevilla, for providing him with this new information. Bernales Ballesteros erroneously relates this document to the sculptural ensemble now preserved in the present-day church of the Magdalena of the convent of San Pablo el Real; see Bernales Ballesteros 1982, 77. In fact, this is a very different ensemble from the one preserved at Olivares, which displays the primitive archaism appropriate to a clearly medieval iconography and which, in contrast to the latter, also incorporates a Saint Joachim that was added later.

15. On this subject, see London 2009–10.

16. Note that Pacheco mentions in his treatise that adherence to this approach was primarily found among "run-of-the-mill" painters, referring to second-rate artists; see Pacheco 1990, 583.

17. Palomino 1947, 894.

18. Tristán appears in documentation in the Stato delle Anime (church census) in the parish of San Lorenzo in Lucina, in the house of the Toledo canon Luigi Ubiedo (Luis Oviedo), as "Luisi pictore," between 1607 and 1609; see Vodret 2011, 68–69.

19. On Tristán's possible sojourn in Seville, see Marías 1992, 141–42. Tristán's annotations on the biography of Pietro Torrigiano in Giorgio Vasari's *Lives of the Most Excellent Painters, Sculptors, and Architects* eloquently help to deduce a direct knowledge of his works in Seville, especially of the Torrigiano *Saint Jerome* now in the Museo de Bellas Artes. The first historian who emphasized the influence on Velázquez of Tristán's *Holy Family* was Martin S. Soria; see Soria 1960, 458. The oldest data regarding the provenance of the *Holy Family* situates it in the sale of Queen Maria Christina's collection at the Hôtel Drouot in Paris (April 16–22, 1879, lot 37). It later passed into the Contini Bonacossi Collection in Florence. See Pérez Sánchez and Navarrete Prieto 2001, 56–58, cat. 49.

20. Navarrete Prieto 2009.

21. Garrido Pérez 1992, 70.

22. On this painting, see Navarrete Prieto 2007b.

Bibliography

Ashley and Sheingorn 1990. Ashley, Kathleen, and Pamela Sheingorn, eds. *Interpreting Cultural Symbols: Saint Anne in Late Medieval Society.* Athens, Ga.: University of Georgia Press, 1990.

Augé 2007. Augé, Jean Louis. "Francisco Pacheco y Diego Velázquez: Del manierismo al naturalismo, ¿Transmisión o transgresión?" In *In Sapientia Libertas: Escritos en homenaje al profesor Alfonso E. Pérez Sánchez,* 255–62. Madrid: Museo Nacional del Prado–Fundación Focus-Abengoa, 2007.

Bassegoda 1999. Bassegoda, Bonaventura. "Pacheco y Velázquez." In Seville 1999. Vol. 2, 124–39.

Benedetti 2005. Benedetti, Sergio. "Alcune osservazioni sugli influssi italiani agli inizi della pittura naturalistica in Spagna." In *Caravaggio e l'Europa: Il movimento caravaggesco internazionale,* 65–74. Exh. cat. Milan: Skira, 2005.

Bergmann 2008. Bergmann, Emilie L. "A Maternal Genealogy of Wisdom: The Education of the Virgin in Early Modern Spanish Iconography." *Confluencia* 24 (2008): 154–61.

Bernales Ballesteros 1982. Bernales Ballesteros, Jorge. *Francisco Antonio Gijón.* Seville: Arte Hispalense, 1982.

Black 2010. Black, Charlene Villaseñor. "Inquisitorial Practices Past and Present: Artistic Censorship, the Virgin Mary, and St. Anne." In *Art, Piety, and Destruction in the Christian West,* 173–200. Ed. Virginia Chieffo Raguin. Burlington, Vt.: Ashgate, 2010.

Brown 1986. Brown, Jonathan. *Velázquez: Painter and Courtier.* New Haven, Conn.: Yale University Press, 1986.

Brown 2010. Brown, Jonathan. "El Velázquez que no era un Velázquez." *ABC,* August 11, 2010. http://www.abc.es/20100810/cultura-arte/velazquez-201008100433.html (accessed May 28, 2014).

Brown and Kagan 1987. Brown, Jonathan, and Richard L. Kagan. "The Duke of Alcalá: His Collection and Its Evolution." *Art Bulletin* 69 (1987): 231–55.

Bruquetas Galán 2002. Bruquetas Galán, Rocío. *Técnicas y materiales de la pintura española en los Siglos de Oro.* Madrid: Fundación de Apoyo a la Historia del Arte Hispánico, 2002.

Ceán Bermúdez 1800. Ceán Bermúdez, J. A. *Diccionario histórico de los más ilustres profesores de las Bellas Artes en España.* 6 vols. Madrid: La Imprenta de la Viuda de Ibarra, 1800.

Cherry 2006. Cherry, Peter. Review of Seville and Bilbao 2005–6. *Burlington Magazine* 148 (2006): 856–57.

Díaz Padrón 2010. Díaz Padrón, Matías. "*La educación de la Virgen* en la Universidad de Yale." *La nueva España,* October 20, 2010. http://www.lne.es/sociedad-cultura/2010/10/20/educacion-virgen-universidad-yale/982907.html (accessed May 28, 2014).

Edinburgh 1996. Davies, David, and Enriqueta Harris. *Velázquez in Seville.* Exh. cat. Edinburgh: National Gallery of Scotland, 1996.

Fallay d'Este 2001. Fallay d'Este, Lauriane. *L'art de la peinture: Peinture et théorie à Séville au temps de Francisco Pacheco.* Paris: Honoré Champion, 2001.

Fernández del Hoyo 2000a. Fernández del Hoyo, María Antonia. "Juan de Roelas, pintor flamenco." *Boletín del Museo Nacional de Escultura* 4 (2000): 24–27.

Fernández del Hoyo 2000b. Fernández del Hoyo, María Antonia. *Pintura y sociedad en Valladolid durante los siglos XVI y XVII.* Valladolid: Academia de la Purísima Concepción, 2000.

Garland 2003. Garland, Patricia Sherwin. *Early Italian Paintings: Approaches to Conservation.* New Haven, Conn.: Yale University Art Gallery, 2003.

Garrido Pérez 1992. Garrido Pérez, Carmen. *Velázquez: Técnica y evolución.* Madrid: Museo Nacional del Prado, 1992.

Gayo and Jover de Celis 2010. Gayo, María Dolores, and Maite Jover de Celis. "Evolución de las preparaciones en la pintura de los siglos XVI y XVII en España." *Boletín del Museo del Prado* 18, no. 46 (2010): 39–59.

Glendinning 1989. Glendinning, Nigel. "Nineteenth-Century British Envoys in Spain and the Taste for Spanish Art in England." *Burlington Magazine* 131 (1989): 117–26.

González de León 1844. González de León, Félix. *Noticia artística de la ciudad de Sevilla.* Seville: Imprenta de José Hidalgo, 1844.

Hale 2005. Hale, Charlotte. "Dating Velázquez's *The Supper at Emmaus.*" *Metropolitan Museum Journal* 40 (2005): 67–77.

Harris 1982. Harris, Enriqueta. *Velázquez.* Oxford: Phaidon, 1982.

Harris 1996. Harris, Enriqueta. "The Question of Velázquez's Assistants." In Edinburgh 1996, 77–78.

Harris 2000. Harris, Enriqueta. Review of Seville 1999. *Burlington Magazine* 142 (2000): 125–27.

Hernández Díaz 1928. Hernández Díaz, José. *Documentos para la historia del arte en Andalucía,* vol. 2. Documentos en Andalucía. Seville: Laboratorio de Arte, Universidad de Sevilla, 1928.

Illán Gutiérrez, Romero Asenjo, and Sáenz de Tejada 2005. Illán Gutiérrez, Adelina, Rafael Romero Asenjo, and Ana Sáenz de Tejada. "Características de las preparaciones sevillanas en pintura de caballete entre 1600 y 1700: Implicaciones en el campo de la restauración de la historia del arte." In *Actas del II Congreso del GEIIC.* Barcelona: Investigación en Conservación y Restauración, 2005. http://ge-iic.com/files/2congresoGE/Caracteristicas_preparaciones_sevillanas.pdf (accessed December 20, 2013).

Keith 2006. Keith, Larry. "Velázquez's Painting Technique." In London 2006–7, 70–89.

Keith and Carr 2009. Keith, Larry, and Dawson W. Carr. "Velázquez's *Christ after the Flagellation*: Technique in Context." *National Gallery Technical Bulletin* 30 (2009): 52–70.

Lleó Cañal 1996. Lleó Cañal, Vicente. "The Cultivated Elite of Velázquez's Seville." In Edinburgh 1996, 23–27.

London 2006–7. Carr, Dawson W., et al. *Velázquez.* Exh. cat. London: National Gallery, 2006.

London and Washington 2009–10. Bray, Xavier, et al. *The Sacred Made Real: Spanish Painting and Sculpture, 1600–1700.* Exh. cat. London: National Gallery, 2009.

Longhi 1951. Longhi, Roberto. "Un Santo Tomás de Velázquez y las conexiones italo-españolas entre los siglos XVI y XVII." *Anales y boletín de los Museos de Arte de Barcelona* 9 (1951): 149–53.

Madrid 2007. Portús Pérez, Javier, ed. *Fábulas de Velázquez: Mitología e historia sagrada en el Siglo de Oro.* Exh. cat. Madrid: Museo Nacional de Prado, 2007.

Madrid 2009. Ruiz Gómez, Leticia, ed. *Juan Batista Maíno, 1581–1649.* Exh. cat. Madrid: Museo Nacional del Prado, 2009.

Marciari 2010. Marciari, John. "Redescubriendo a Velázquez/Velázquez Rediscovered: *The Education of the Virgin* at Yale." *Ars Magazine* 7 (2010): 52–66, 149–53.

Marciari 2012. Marciari, John. Review of Rome 2011–12, and *Il Rinascimento a Roma: Nel segno di Michelangelo e Raffaello,* by Maria Grazia Bernardini and Marco Bussagli. *Tabula Quarterly* (Winter 2012). http://tabulaquarterly.com/winter-2012.php#review2 (accessed May 28, 2014).

Marciari 2013a. Marciari, John. Review of *Diego Velázquez: The Early Court Portraits*, by Javier Portús Pérez et al. *Burlington Magazine* 155 (2013): 291–92.

Marciari 2013b. Marciari, John. Review of Tiffany 2012. *Burlington Magazine* 155 (2013): 710.

Marciari 2013c. Marciari, John. "Zurbarán en América/Zurbarán in America." *Ars Magazine* 20 (2013): 24–36, 142–44.

Marías 1992. Marías, Fernando. "Las anotaciones de Luis Tristán a las Vidas de Vasari." In Fernando Marías and Xavier de Salas, *El Greco y el arte de su tiempo: Las notas de El Greco a Vasari*, 139–43. Madrid: Real Fundación de Toledo, 1992.

Marini 1981. Marini, Maurizio. "Del Signor Giovanni Battista Crescentij, Pittore." *J. Paul Getty Museum Journal* 9 (1981): 127–32.

Martínez Chumillas 1948. Martínez Chumillas, Manuel. *Alonso Cano*. Madrid: Editorial Carlos Jaime, 1948.

Massing 2012. Massing, Anne. *Painting Restoration before La Restauration: The Origins of the Profession in France*. London: Harvey Miller, 2012.

McKim-Smith 1979. McKim-Smith, Gridley. "On Velázquez's Working Method." *Art Bulletin* 61 (December 1979): 589–603.

McKim-Smith 1999. McKim-Smith, Gridley. "La técnica sevillana de Velázquez." In Seville 1999. Vol. 2, 108–23.

McKim-Smith and Newman 1993. McKim-Smith, Gridley, and Richard Newman. *Ciencia e historia del arte: Velázquez en el Prado*. Madrid: Museo Nacional del Prado, 1993.

McKim-Smith et al. 2005. McKim-Smith, Gridley, et al. "Velázquez: Painting from Life." *Metropolitan Museum Journal* 40 (2005): 79–91.

Morales 2004. Morales, Alfredo J., et al. *Guía artística de Sevilla y su provincia*. 2 vols. 2nd ed. Seville: Diputación de Sevilla, Fundación José Manuel Lara, 2004.

Muñoz 2008. Muñoz, Valme. "Santa Ana enseñando a leer a la Virgen." In Seville 2008–9, 170–72.

Navarrete Prieto 2007a. Navarrete Prieto, Benito. "La aportación de Pablo de Céspedes al primer naturalismo en Sevilla: Juan de Roelas y Francisco de Herrera el Viejo." In *In Sapientia Libertas: Escritos en homenaje al profesor Alfonso E. Pérez Sánchez*, 247–54. Madrid: Museo Nacional del Prado–Fundación Focus-Abengoa, 2007.

Navarrete Prieto 2007b. Navarrete Prieto, Benito. "*La Sagrada Parentela* de Francisco de Herrera el Viejo en la Galería española de Louis-Philippe." *Museo de Bellas Artes de Bilbao* 3 (2007): 75–100.

Navarrete Prieto 2009. Navarrete Prieto, Benito. "Velázquez y Sevilla: *La Inmaculada* del Deán López Cepero recuperada." *Ars Magazine* 3 (2009): 100–117.

Navarrete Prieto 2010. Navarrete Prieto, Benito. "Entender al primer Velázquez." *El país*, October 20, 2010, 31.

Nixon 2004. Nixon, Virginia. *Mary's Mother: Saint Anne in Late Medieval Europe*. University Park, Pa.: Penn State University Press, 2004.

Pacheco 1990. Pacheco, Francisco. *Arte de la pintura* (1649). Ed. Bonaventura Bassegoda i Hugas. Madrid: Cátedra, 1990.

Palomino 1947. Palomino, Acisclo Antonio. *El museo pictórico y escala óptica con el parnaso español pintoresco laureado*. Madrid: M. Aguilar, 1947.

Passolas Jáuregui 1997. Passolas Jáuregui, Jaime. *Curiosidades, leyendas y tradiciones de las iglesias y conventos de Sevilla*. Seville: CB Ediciones, 1997.

Pérez Sánchez 1968. Pérez Sánchez, Alfonso E. "La crisis de la pintura española en el año 1600." In *España en las crisis del arte europeo*, 167–77. Madrid: CSIC, Instituto Diego Velázquez, 1968.

Pérez Sánchez and Navarrete Prieto 2001. Pérez Sánchez, Alfonso E., and Benito Navarrete Prieto. *Luis Tristán, h. 1585–1624*. Madrid: Real Fundación Toledo, 2001.

Pericolo 2011. Pericolo, Lorenzo. *Caravaggio and Pictorial Narrative: Dislocating the "Istoria" in Early Modern Painting*. London: Harvey Miller, 2011.

Ponz 1947. Ponz, Antonio. *Viaje de España* (1789). Madrid: M. Aguilar, 1947.

Portús Pérez 2009. Portús Pérez, Javier. "San Juan Bautista en el desierto y el canon del joven Velázquez." *Ars Magazine* 2 (2009): 54–67.

Reist and Colomer 2012. Reist, Inge, and José Luis Colomer, eds. *Collecting Spanish Art: Spain's Golden Age and America's Gilded Age*. New York: Frick Collection, 2012.

Rome 2011–12. Vodret, Rossella, ed. *Roma al tempo di Caravaggio, 1600–1630*. Exh. cat. Milan: Skira, 2011.

Serrera 1984. Serrera, Juan Miguel. "Pinturas y pintores del siglo XVI en la catedral de Sevilla." In *La catedral de Sevilla*, 353–404. Seville: Guadalquivir, 1984.

Serrera 1996. Serrera, Juan Miguel. "Velázquez and Sevillian Painting of His Time." In Edinburgh 1996, 37–43.

Seville 1999. Morales, Alfredo J., et al. *Velázquez y Sevilla: Monasterio de la Cartuja de Santa María de las Cuevas, Salas del Centro Andaluz de Arte Contemporáneo, Sevilla, del 1 de octubre al 12 de diciembre de 1999*. Exh. cat. 2 vols. Seville: Junta de Andalucía, Consejería de Cultura, 1999.

Seville 2008–9. Valdivieso González, Enrique, and Ignacio Cano Rivero, eds. *Juan de Roelas, h. 1570–1625*. Exh. cat. Seville: Junta de Andalucía, Consejería de Cultura, 2008.

Seville and Bilbao 2005–6. Pérez Sánchez, Alfonso E., and Benito Navarrete Prieto, eds. *De Herrera a Velázquez: El primer naturalismo en Sevilla*. Exh. cat. Seville: Fundación Focus-Abengoa, 2005.

Sheingorn 1993. Sheingorn, Pamela. "'The Wise Mother': The Image of St. Anne Teaching the Virgin Mary." *Gesta* 32 (1993): 69–80.

Soria 1960. Soria, Martin S. "Velázquez y Tristán." In *Varia Velazqueña: Homenaje a Velázquez en el III centenario de su muerte, 1660–1960*. Vol. 1, 456–62. Madrid: Ministerio de Educación Nacional, Dirección General de Bellas Artes, 1960.

Tiffany 2012. Tiffany, Tanya. *Diego Velázquez's Early Paintings and the Culture of Seventeenth-Century Seville*. University Park, Pa.: Penn State University Press, 2012.

Turin 2005–6. Sanguineti, Daniele. *Bartolomeo Cavarozzi: "Sacre Familie" a confronto*. Exh. cat. Milan: Skira, 2005.

Valdivieso González 1978. Valdivieso González, Enrique. *Juan de Roelas*. Seville: Diputación Provincial de Sevilla, 1978.

Valdivieso González and Serrera 1985. Valdivieso González, Enrique, and Juan Miguel Serrera. *Historia de la pintura española: Escuela sevillana del primer tercio del siglo XVI*. Madrid: Centro de Estudios Históricos, 1985.

Véliz 1996. Véliz, Zahira. "Velázquez's Early Technique." In Edinburgh 1996, 79–95.

Vodret 2011. Vodret, Rossella. *Alla ricerca di "Ghiongrat": Studi sui libri parrochiali romani (1600–1630)*. Rome: "L'Erma" di Bretschneider, 2011.

Wethey 1955. Wethey, Harold E. *Alonso Cano: Painter, Sculptor, Architect*. Princeton, N.J.: Princeton University Press, 1955.

Zuccari, Véliz, and Fiedler 2005. Zuccari, Frank, Zahira Véliz, and Inge Fiedler. "Saint John in the Wilderness: Observations on Technique, Style, Authorship." *Museum Studies* 31, no. 2 (2005): 30–45, 105–8.

Photo Credits

Every effort has been made to credit the artists
and the sources; if there are errors or omissions,
please contact the Yale University Art Gallery
so that corrections can be made in any
subsequent editions.

Photograph © The Art Institute of Chicago:
    Marciari, fig. 5
© Bilboko Arte Ederren Museoa-Museo de
    Bellas Artes de Bilbao: Navarrete Prieto,
    fig. 10
© English Heritage: Marciari, fig. 2
© Fundación Focus-Abengoa, Sevilla. Fotografía:
    José Abaurre: Navarrete Prieto, fig. 6
Image © The Metropolitan Museum of Art.
    Image source: Art Resource, N.Y. Photo:
    Malcolm Varon: Marciari, fig. 4
Minneapolis Institute of Arts: pl. 3; Navarrete
    Prieto, figs. 4–5
© José Morón Borrego: Navarrete Prieto, pl. 4;
    figs. 1–3, 8
Cliché Musée des Beaux-Arts d'Orléans:
    Marciari, fig. 7
Courtesy Museo de Bellas Artes de Sevilla/
    © José Morón Borrego: pl. 2
© National Gallery, London/Art Resource, N.Y.:
    Marciari, figs. 6, 8
© Patrimonio Nacional: Marciari, fig. 9
Photograph: A. Roy, courtesy of National
    Gallery, London: Albendea, McClure,
    Bezur, and Stenger, fig. 4
Scottish National Gallery: Marciari, fig. 3
Photograph © The State Hermitage Museum.
    Photo by Vladimir Terebenin, Leonard
    Kheifets, Yuri Molodkovets: Marciari, fig. 1
Yale University Art Gallery Archives, New
    Haven, Conn.: Marciari, fig. 10
© Yale University Art Gallery, New Haven,
    Conn., Conservation Department:
Albendea, McClure, Bezur, and Stenger,
    figs. 2, 5–11, 13–14; Navarrete Prieto, fig. 7
Yale University Art Gallery, New Haven, Conn.,
    Visual Resources Department: pl. 1;
    Albendea, McClure, Bezur, and Stenger,
    figs. 1, 3, 12; Navarrete Prieto, fig. 9